A GIFT
of GRACE

The Essence of
Guru Nanak's Spirituality

Daler Aashna Deol

NIYOGI
BOOKS

Published by
NIYOGI BOOKS
Block D, Building No. 77,
Okhla Industrial Area, Phase-I,
New Delhi-110 020, INDIA
Tel: 91-11-26816301, 26818960
Email: niyogibooks@gmail.com
Website: www.niyogibooksindia.com

Text © Daler Aashna Deol

Editor: Sukanya Sur
Cover Design: Nabanita Das/ Kaushikee
Layout: Nabanita Das

ISBN: 978-93-89136-16-6
Publication: 2019

Printed at: Niyogi Offset Pvt. Ltd., New Delhi, India

Contents

Part III: Selected Hymns of Guru Nanak (153–226)

Preface

He spoke of love and compassion for all. He saw in the skies not only stars but the worlds beyond our world in an endless loop—an idea that his contemporaries could not fully comprehend. He called upon his followers to burn worldly love and think of the love that is endless and eternal. He knew that sickness in the human heart is not a common disease but a condition caused by our indifference to spiritual life. It is an eternal agony that is cured only by the love of the Lord, the Creator and sustainer of this universe. When we forget Him, we go astray and miss the opportunity to gain enlightenment in this life, which is a precious gift. He told his listeners that the sacred word (*shabad*) is a priceless pearl, and, when not used, it slips out of our grip and is hard to get back. He implored people around him, 'Love the Lord as lotus loves water.' Get thirsty for the Name. He compared himself to a *papiha* (a songbird that is known to call for rain), seeking the water of God's mercy. Our life, he said, is like a long and sleepless night. There is only one source of light and grace—*Ek Onkaar Sat Naam* (One True Name). Don't wander all alone in the wilderness. Don't try to swim in the turbulent sea on your own. Seek help from the One, the Only One. He will tell you how to find pearls in the ocean, how to transform your ordinary mind into a temple, and how to end the sorrow of your soul permanently.

He was Guru Nanak, born in 1469 in a modest Hindu family, who founded one of the newest world religions. He wrote 976 hymns and other compositions in 19 ragas that are exceptional in their poetic beauty and spiritual depth. This book simplifies Guru Nanak's message for the modern reader. Some of the foundational themes found in the first part of this work include love and compassion for fellow human beings, being a caring member of the family and the community to which one belongs, charitable giving, caring for and working to retain nature's beauty and environment, and maintaining a regular practice of name recitation (*naam simran*).

Japji Sahib, which is the seminal text and the very centre of Guru Nanak's spiritual legacy, is included in its entirety in the second part of the book. Each meditation is presented as transliterated text, followed by its English translation and a brief commentary. Besides *Japji Sahib*, this book includes in the third part a representative selection of Guru Nanak's sacred hymns (*shabad*s), which were written in a soulful musical language and infused with the spirit of enlightenment. They contain profound insights into establishing connection with the loving God and are a vital source of the message of love and compassion.

Both *Japji Sahib* and the sacred hymns are textually challenging works to render in another language. The beauty and depth of their meaning, together with a lyrical depiction of hymns based on different Indian ragas, are hard to retain in translation as one tries to save the tonal quality of the original text. Though an effort has been made to match the depth of meaning and aural experience of the original, no such attempt is likely to yield a perfect result. And this one does not. If the reader comes to understand and appreciate the essence of Guru Nanak's spirituality from this book, it will be a great reward for me.

This book includes material that was first presented in *Japji: The Path of Devotional Meditation*, a book that I co-authored with my husband Surinder Deol, and which was published in USA in 1998. I want to express my thanks to Surinder for his help and guidance in the writing of this book, and revision of some of the previously published text. Following a spiritual tradition is like building a bridge that narrows distances and brings people together—something that is urgently needed in our meaninglessly violent and chaotic world. It is a challenge to follow the spiritual path while leading a material and competitive life in a modern society with all its distractions. This book aims to make your task easy and enjoyable.

PART I
THE SPIRITUAL FOUNDATION

Devotional Meditation

Contemplate in the name of God solely—
Fruitless is all other ritual.

[Raga Suhi]

G uru Nanak preached the path of total devotion, in which recitation of the Name (*naam simran*) is a form of meditation. According to a survey by Daniel Goleman,[1] the root of devotional paths can be traced to ancient classics such as *Srimad Bhagavatam,* which recommended chanting the name of Sri Krishna. Recitation of the Name is also advocated in many other spiritual traditions. The Koran contains the ninety-nine most beautiful names of Allah. Sufis use these names in what they call 'remembrance'—a time of intense meditation. Christians offer prayers in the name of Jesus Christ, remembering him as the son of God. Buddhists make use of mantras such as *Om Ah Hum Vajra Guru Padma Siddhi Hum* (the embodiment of the body, speech, and mind of the Buddhas, O Padmasambhava, please grant all blessings).

Devotional meditation originates in the heart and soul of a devotee, and is directed outward to a higher being (the flow of feeling and emotions is from the subject to the object). For the performer, it is what transpersonal psychologists call a 'peak' experience, in which one is elevated from the immediate surroundings and transported to a world of soul consciousness.

---

1 Daniel Goleman, *The Meditative Mind: The Varieties of Meditative Experience* (New York: TarcherPerigee Books, 1988). [The book was originally published in 1977 as *The Varieties of Meditative Experience.*]

People often ask, how can reciting a name, chanting a mantra, singing a *shabad*, or participating in a kirtan make any difference? It is a valid question. There are three answers. First, recitation of a sacred word, such as Om, Jesus, Allah, or Ek Onkaar, concentrates our mind like nothing else, and narrows down our attention on the object of recitation. For example, if we say *Waheguru* (the most popular description of God among Sikhs, which means 'greetings to the greatest guru of all beings'), we direct our gratitude and salutation to a single source of cosmic energy that is very difficult to visualize in normal course. The picture that emerges in our mind is not the picture of an individual being but of the whole cosmic sphere. Once we hear the Name, we have an opportunity to engage in some creative imagery of our own. We can elevate ourselves mentally. We can try to picture in our mind how the Supreme Being might look. We can see the 'sound and light show' of the universe in perpetual motion, while reflecting on the unbreakable bond between the Creator and His Creation.

Second, recitation of the Name bridges the gulf between the individual and the deity. It can turn quickly into a creative dialogue or conversation, whereby the deity speaks to the individual and provides answers to tough questions. For a person of deep faith, it is the voice of the inner self. But in order to listen to this voice, whether it comes from inside or outside, we have to be in touch with our higher self.

Third, recitation of the Name is also a form of meditation and confers all the benefits associated with meditation. But it needs to be said that Nanak does not recommend deep and socially isolating meditative practices common in Hinduism and Buddhism. The best meditation is the recitation of the Name in the solitude of one's home or in the company of other believers. Nanak's spirituality is deeply rooted in the family and the community. Therefore, the practitioner is empowered to have a 'peak' experience as well as a 'plateau' experience (sharing one's spiritual pursuits with family, friends, and community).

Guru Nanak's Life and Work

An understanding of the mystical significance of the Guru's teachings requires a brief introduction to his life and the core of his message. He was born on 15 April 1469[1], in a village near Lahore, now in Pakistan. The place was later renamed Nankana Sahib in the Guru's memory. Most accounts of the Guru's life are based on contemporary hagiographical sketches (*janam sakhis*) written for pedagogical purposes. As a precocious child, Nanak uttered words of wisdom that were beyond the understanding of people around him. The family priest, who read his horoscope, predicted that both Hindus and Muslims will revere him. His name will be known on earth and in heaven. As he walks, the ocean will part to give him way. So will the earth and the sky. He will worship and acknowledge only the Supreme Being, and he will command others to do the same.

Nanak, as a student, surprised his teachers with his sharp and philosophic mind. Married at the age of sixteen, he had two sons. It soon became clear that young Nanak did not have much interest in the material reality of a householder's life. His sister invited him

---

1   Guru Nanak's birth account is available in various traditional histories known as *janamsakhi*s. It was agreed by hagiographers that the Guru was born in the month of Vaisakh (April). But during Maharaja Ranjit Singh's reign, based on the judgement of a court historian, the birth celebration was moved to Kattak or Kartik (which is October–November) to bring it closer to Diwali. Thus, a new practice was established and it continued during the British rule. SGPC (the highest Sikh religious authority) has officially declared 15 April 1469 as the birth date of Guru Nanak, although the practice of celebrating it in October–November (the first full moon following Diwali) has been allowed to continue.

to move to Sultanpur, and persuaded her husband to get him a job with the local nawab. As the job involved only mundane accounting, Nanak spent most of his time on his search for the True One.

In August 1507, the spiritual Nanak had a mystical experience involving a revelation while bathing in the Bein River. After three days, he emerged from the river as a messiah, chanting that there is neither Hindu nor Muslim. His acquaintances were taken by surprise, who had given up on him as drowned. After this great transformational event of self-enlightenment, he was always addressed as Guru Nanak. The Guru subsequently set out on a long journey of discovery, that took him to several of Hindu pilgrimages within India and also to the sacred Muslim cities of Mecca and Medina.

It is difficult to account for the significant influences on the Guru's life, but he shared many of his beliefs with those in mystical and devotional traditions that produced saints like Kabir. There is no evidence to corroborate guesses regarding the Guru's meeting with Kabir, although there is some possibility that they were contemporaries. The Guru witnessed the brutal tyranny of Mughal Emperor Babur's invasion of India and wrote about it. The last part of the Guru's life was spent in Kartarpur, where he laid the institutional foundation of the Sikh faith. *Japji Sahib* (The Morning Prayer) was written during this period.

The Guru joined his Supreme Beloved on 22 September 1539. The following account of this event appears in Puratan text: 'Guru Baba Nanak then went and sat under a withered acacia, which immediately produced leaves and flowers, becoming verdant again. Guru Angad (his principal disciple and the successor) prostrated himself ... The assembled congregation sang hymns of praise, and Baba Nanak passed into an ecstatic trance. While thus transported, and in obedience to the divine will, he sang the hymn entitled *Bara Maah* (*The Twelve Months*). It was early morning and the time had come for his final departure....

'Hindus and Muslims, who had put their faith in the Divine Name began to debate what should be done with the Guru's body. "We shall bury him," said the Muslims. "No, let us cremate his body," said the Hindus. "Place flowers on both sides of my body," said Baba Nanak, "flowers from the Hindus on the right side and flowers from the Muslims on the left. If tomorrow the Hindus' flowers are still fresh let my body be burned, and if the Muslims' flowers are still fresh let it be buried."

' ... Baba Nanak then covered himself with a sheet and passed away. Those who had gathered around him prostrated themselves, and when the sheet was removed, they found that there was nothing under it. The flowers on both sides remained fresh, and both Hindus and Muslims took their respective shares.'[2]

---

2   Adapted from W.H. McLeod, trans. and ed., *Textual Sources for the Study of Sikhism* (Chicago: The University of Chicago Press, 1984), p. 25.

Guru Nanak and Hinduism

G uru Nanak was born into and lived in a social and cultural environment that was predominantly Hindu in its beliefs and practices. Hinduism, a denomination drawn from a Persian word, is a complex set of beliefs, doctrines, and practices. It is a mixture of religion, philosophy, and culture. All Sikhs are followers of Guru Nanak, but the Guru has a sizeable following outside of the Sikh community as well. Many Hindus show reverence to Guru Nanak as an incarnate saint.

We need to note three principal differences. First, Guru Nanak preaches a strictly monotheistic faith, whereas Hinduism, in theory, is monotheistic in the sense that there is a unified concept of God, Brahma, or the Ultimate Reality. In practice, however, Hindus worship several gods and goddesses, treating them more or less as autonomous beings.

Second, Guru Nanak makes spirituality a family-centred pursuit that encourages people to lead a spiritual life, while also fulfilling their communal and societal obligations. In Guru Nanak's theology, there is no concept of *sanyas* (giving up domestic life). Enlightenment needs to be pursued while being a model householder.

Third, Guru Nanak firmly believes in the equality of all human beings, who are capable of attaining moksha or spiritual liberation. As a consequence, he rejects both the caste system and the priestly power that sustains the caste system.

There are many areas of agreement between the traditional Hindu faith and the path preached by Guru Nanak. For one, Hindus believe in three distinct paths to liberation, namely the path of knowledge (*jnana yoga*), the path of devotion (*bhakti yoga*), and the path of action (*karma yoga*). Guru Nanak regards all three paths as legitimate ways of attaining spiritual enlightenment, but considers the path of devotion, coupled with moral living, as more potent and practical. Guru Nanak's hymns are highly devotional in content; he also emphasizes the need for leading a virtuous life.

In another area of agreement, Guru Nanak accepts the doctrine of karma, which says that we are rewarded or punished in the next life based on the quality of our actions in this life. Liberation (moksha) means cessation of the cycle of life and death.

There is an agreement also in that Guru Nanak's faith and Hinduism share many aspects of social, cultural, and religious life. For instance, Guru Nanak's followers show reverence to Hindu gods and goddesses and accept them as manifestations of the One Supreme Being, which has been elaborately described by Guru Nanak in his work. Many Hindu and Sikh festivals are common. Diwali, the festival of lights, is celebrated in both religions, though for somewhat different reasons. Sikhs have the same aversion to eating beef as Hindus. In fact, vegetarianism is a requirement in both religions, although it is unevenly practiced. Marriages between Hindu and Sikh families are commonplace. Guru Nanak and Hinduism subscribe to identical creation myths. For Guru Nanak, this universe is the creation of God; for Hindus, it is the work of the Divine, manifested as Lord Brahma.

Guru Nanak shares with traditional Hinduism the four goals of life: righteousness (*dharma*), economic success (*artha*), pleasure in married life (*kama*), and spiritual enlightenment (*moksha*). There is, however, great emphasis by Guru Nanak on the importance of divine grace as a prerequisite for liberation.

Guru Nanak's vision of human beings is strongly egalitarian. All human beings, irrespective of caste, colour, creed, or gender, must be treated equally as moral beings, transcending these distinctions. The

Hindu society of his time was divided into different castes. Only the highest class (Brahmins) was qualified to read the scriptures. People from the lowest level were not entitled to hear the word of God. Guru Nanak believes in the equality of all human beings—no difference should exist due to gender, colour, race, and living style. Women in Indian society are frequently treated as inferior to men, with no capacity for independent, creative, or spiritual pursuits. On the role of women in religion and culture, Guru Nanak had strong views:

> From woman is a man born, inside her is he conceived;
> to a woman is a man engaged and a woman he marries.
> A woman is man's companion.
> From woman originates new generations.
> Should woman die, another is solicited;
> by woman's help is man kept in restraint.
> Why revile her of whom are born great ones of the earth?
> From woman is born a woman, no human being without a woman is born.
> Only True Lord, says Nanak, is without a woman.
>
> [Raga Asa]

Although several Hindu scriptures (including the Vedas) did not sanction a caste system based on heredity, the social structure of four classes had solidified to such an extent that heredity had become civil society's sole organizing principle. The Guru broke this hierarchy of the caste system and conceptualized only one class of humans who lived under the care and protection of one loving God.

According to Guru Nanak, no man or woman is a fallen being. We are all capable of leading a moral life. The Guru's conception of a virtuous life consists of human beings resisting the five dreadful streams of fire, which are propensities or springs of action, namely lust, greed, attachment, anger, and pride. These forces become dominant when our mind is not under our control. These evils are overcome by recitation of the Name. As fire is put out by water, so the Name frees us from these limiting propensities.

The Guru considered the established priestly order as highly corrupt and morally decadent. Priests did not practice what they preached. They did not understand the meaning of scriptures that they mechanically used to promote their message. They encouraged the perpetuation of practices and rituals that did not bear any spiritual fruit. The Guru exposed the hollowness of some of these rituals. Instead of doing any good, they were harmful to people's spiritual growth because they took them away from God.

According to Guru Nanak, a holy life can be pursued in the course of our ordinary life—being a householder, earning a rightful living, and meeting the challenges of daily life. It was another departure from the Hindu way of life wherein human life was divided into four episodes— *brahmacharya* (the student life), *grihastha* (the family life), *vanaprastha* (retirement from the working life), and *sanyas* (a life free from all worldly attachments). Guru Nanak advocates leading an exemplary life based on good education, a married life built around love and mutual respect, moral and ethical upbringing of children, and retired life of active community service, prayer, and meditation.

Guru Nanak and Buddhism

Although it is uncommon to find parallels between Guru Nanak and Gautama Buddha, there are many similarities. Both Gautama Buddha and Guru Nanak preached new paths that challenged the established order; both questioned all forms of ritualism; both spoke to ordinary people in a language that they understood; both warned their disciples against blind following of tradition; both advocated the importance of rightful livelihood; both preached equality between all individuals and between men and women; both pushed the middle road, a path that avoids the extremes of asceticism and indulgence; and both spoke about a life of infinite compassion and enlightenment that comes from within oneself.

The basic teaching of Buddhism is found in the Four Noble Truths: this life is characterized by suffering; suffering is caused by craving, desire, and attachment; pain can cease because its cause can cease; and the path of truth that leads to cessation of suffering is the Eightfold Path—right understanding, right thought (these two conditions lead to wisdom), right speech, right action, right livelihood (these three conditions constitute morality), right effort, right mindfulness, and right concentration (the last three conditions lead to increased focus or samadhi).

In Guru Nanak's hymns, there is repeated emphasis on many of the same things included in the Eightfold Path, but the Guru takes a much more optimistic view of life than Gautama Buddha. First, according to Guru Nanak, life has suffering as well as happiness and bliss depending on the choices made by us. This life is an opportunity to show devotion to our Creator and to pray for divine blessings. This life is also the start of our spiritual journey. Second, Guru Nanak commends the path of devotion, with remembrance of the Name as its central discipline, and not the way of intense meditation recommended by Buddhism. Third, in the Eightfold Path, there is no appeal to divine grace, which is an essential prerequisite for completing the spiritual journey described by Guru Nanak. Fourth, unlike Guru Nanak, Buddhism has no concept of God as the Supreme Being. Most Buddhist deities are spirits that are conditioned by their actions, and, as such, are not yet fully liberated.

In spite of these differences, there is much common ground between Guru Nanak and Buddhism, not only on spiritual beliefs but also on social organization. Guru Nanak's conception of *sangat* (a congregation of like-minded souls) is not very different from the Buddhist sangha (a religious community), where the Buddhist way of life is practiced.

Guru Nanak and Islam

Guru Nanak gives the impression of being a Sufi, in the sense that he was deeply in love with his Creator, and his hymns have the same mystical quality found in the inspired poetry of Sufi saints. He celebrates the beauty and grandeur of the Supreme Beloved in the tradition of Sufi saints, such as Attar and Rumi. Also, the hymns of Muslim Sufi saints like Sheikh Farid were included in the *Sri Guru Granth Sahib* along with the hymns of Sikh gurus and Hindu saints. In one of his compositions, Guru Nanak debated the question of being a true Muslim. He wrote:

> Make the mosque of compassion your prayer mat;
> make honest living your motto, as the Koran says.
> Let modesty be your circumcision, and noble path your
> Ramadan fast—
> Such a Muslim you ought to be!
> Let good work be your Kaaba, and truth your prophet;
> let good actions be your affirmation and prayer; let your rosary
> please God.
> Only then, says Nanak, your honor before God be vindicated.
>
> [Raga Majh]

Guru Nanak respected the core of Islam as a true religion, based on divine revelation to the Prophet. Many Muslim saints showed respect to Guru Nanak during his life as a truly enlightened soul.

There is a view that Guru Nanak created a synthesis of the best in Hinduism and Islam. There is no concrete evidence to support this thesis. If anything, Sikhism owes its origin to the spiritual enlightenment of its founder, who wanted to transcend the institutionalized traditional differences among people based solely on their religion. Nanak said that there is neither Hindu nor Muslim. We are all children of one God, who is our sole provider and protector, and we owe our unqualified allegiance to that one Supreme Deity.

The Nature of God

According to Guru Nanak, God is formless and unfathomable yet gracious and loving. God, as the ultimate preceptor, speaks through saints from time to time. Guru Nanak was one of those saints. His lyrical verses enable us to know the unknowable through his own spiritual experiences. Recitation of the sacred Name, which is the quintessential experience of reading or listening to God's word, removes the need for all other actions.

For saints in the devotional tradition, a tradition marked by selfless love, God exists either without attributes or with attributes, that is, in human form. Guru Nanak's conception of God is unambiguous. Belief in one God is the first principle of his devotion, but it is also devotion for a God that is formless, immortal, beyond the cycle of life and death, self-illumined, and true. This view is strongly without attributes; therefore, it should not be confused with the worship of a personal god. The Guru's emphasis on listening to recitation of the Name acknowledges that God's unseen presence can be encountered at a very personal level. Although God is not manifest, there is divine presence in our daily life. The most significant manifestation of God is in the medium of the holy word that is revealed to a preceptor, who then shares it with the rest of humanity.

Five Stages of the Spiritual Journey

All human beings, with some initial preparation, are capable of undertaking the spiritual journey. In meditations (*pauris*) 34 through 37 of *Japji Sahib*, Guru Nanak describes five separate and distinct stages of the spiritual journey: the first stage is that of moral living and rightful action (*dharam khand*). It is the playing field for the principles of conventional morality. If we abide by the accepted religious and moral principles common to all religions, and can differentiate between good and evil, we may find ourselves at the start of a journey that eventually takes us closer to God.

The second stage is that of divine knowledge (*jnan khand*). In this realm, one relentlessly searches for mystical and spiritual awareness. Real knowledge pertains to the nature of God, the origin of the universe, cosmic laws, the purpose of human life, and the central role of the Creator in keeping this vast creation in balance. Once we enter this realm, the mysteries of creation are revealed to us.

The third stage is that of spiritual beauty, effort, and unfoldment (*saram khand*), in which one develops the spiritual strength to see beyond material reality and gain spiritual expansion. The spirit is steeped in unparalleled aesthetic experiences. Beauty is generally considered an attribute of the human body. But the beauty of the mind or soul is an unfoldment in a different dimension. It is sheer radiance produced by the human mind when an ocean of divine light embraces it. In this realm, the spirit truly transforms itself and prepares to realize its potential.

The fourth stage is that of divine grace (*karam khand*). An endless flow of higher energy is opened for the chosen few who reach this point. Not everyone is worthy of divine grace. Grace is the sovereign prerogative of the Supreme. We can pray for it but can't demand it. Grace is a gift, a reward, but not a personal accomplishment.

The fifth and last stage is that of eternal truth (*sach khand*), representing the centre of God's formless state and of creation itself. In this realm are infinite places of heavenly beauty, wherein reside fully realized beings who have successfully made the transition from the lower to the upper realms. It is the stage of total self-realization and unity of consciousness.

Building a Spiritually Nourishing Relationship with God

We can establish a spiritually nourishing relationship with God only after we understand what God really is. God is One. The concept of the oneness of God is familiar to many spiritual traditions. In the Bible, the Lord declares, 'Beside me, there is no God,' and 'There is no God but one' (Isaiah 45:5). According to the Koran, God is not *a* God but *the* God. In Confucianism, God is equated with absolute truth. In Buddhism, the essential, universal, and undifferentiated quality of Ultimate Reality is called 'suchness', which, among other things, means truth (oneness). In *Vishnu Purana*, a sacred Hindu scripture, Brahma, Vishnu, and Shiva are represented as chief energies of Brahman (God), a view similar to that extended by Guru Nanak: all gods and goddesses are manifestations of one true God, who alone is supreme.

As a source of compassion and grace, God transcends all distinctions of time and place. Some philosophers have looked upon God as a source of what is right and good. There are those who have called God the 'eternal mystery', and others claim to have intimate knowledge of the Supreme through simple faith and daily prayer. Many proofs have been offered to show that God exists. These maintain, for example, that if this world is real, with its amazing landscape, its creator must also exist. If there is purpose and order in the universe, as we, no doubt, find at all times, it could not have been possible without a higher force managing it. If we believe that our life has a potential for spiritual experience, there must be a definite source of this goodness.

Guru Nanak equates God with truth, a view also shared by St. Thomas Aquinas, who wrote that truth has its source in God. It means that what is true cannot be challenged and can never be falsified. It describes the everlasting reality known through faith, not reason. Our experience of true living is a divine experience. It is through this experience that we come closer to the True Name. The Guru, as a spiritual guide, in this context, is a mediator of divine truth.

Truth is a fundamental, divine attribute and distinguishes the Supreme Being from all other beings or created objects. It demands perfection, which is not possible through the free play of natural forces, or through human birth, which is another step in our quest for perfection. Only the Creator can be above all imperfections, impurities, and falsifications. When we depart from truth (as the revealed word of God), we move away from God.

God is above fear of any kind. Fear is a part of our daily life. We are afraid of being harmed; we are scared that our loved ones will be hurt. More than anything else, we are scared of being sick, losing our wealth or job, and, above all, of dying. Fear is the recognition that there is a power bigger than us and more brutal than us that can harm us. The harm may be physical or psychological. As long as it lasts, it takes tremendous emotional toll because it exerts pressure on our nervous system, on our reflexes, and on our ability to think clearly. God is above fear because nothing exists that is not a part of the divine creation. The source of anxiety, to be credible, has to have a life of its own. What is mortal cannot be a source of worry or concern to one who is immortal.

God is the ultimate source of love and compassion. Love captures all fear. Compassion destroys all evil, not through any violent reaction but as a fountain of light that slowly conquers all darkness. Once we get closer to God, we move away from fear. In short, despair is a reflection of our imperfect divinity. Once our life is filled with divine love, fear departs. Where love resides, fear has no place. Alternatively, when love disappears, fear takes over. God is without malice, jealousy, or ill will. Love is God's vital attribute—He loves all beings and created phenomena. When the

Supreme Beloved is itself a fountain of love, feelings of hatred, malice, jealousy, or ill will have no place in the divine realm. But in our own life, these things do matter, often creating a field of negative energy around us. When we open ourselves to God, we experience an unstoppable shower of love. We cleanse ourselves of all negativities.

The Bible says, 'We love because He first loved us' (1 John 4:19). In Guru Nanak's spirituality, love is not only an ideal but also a matter of daily practice. If there is no kindness in our hearts, we have no divinity left, and we are no different from an animal. To practice what we preach, we need to express our love in selfless service to others. The Guru says that without selfless service, no lofty objective can be fulfilled; only when we serve selflessly can we earn the merit of pure action.

Love knows no calculation. It does not ask for anything in return. In one of his compositions, Guru Nanak makes the point that a true lover is merely absorbed in the love of the Beloved. If the Beloved does not respond, no complaint or frustration is expressed. Such a claim is frivolous because God's love for us is never in question. If we don't feel it within, we have not looked far enough or deep enough. To receive love, we have to make a gift of love. Giving is receiving; we are getting back what we offer, but not many of us look at love this way.

Forgiveness is another form of love. Forgiving wrongs opens our heart to someone who needs love. Sheikh Farid, a Sufi saint, whose poetical work is included in *Sri Guru Granth Sahib*, says:

Those who beat you with fists,
do not pay them in the same coin.
Before leaving, kiss their feet.

God, according to Guru Nanak, is formless and, thus, timeless. Formlessness is not the same thing as emptiness. Formlessness, in reality, is a higher consciousness—a simultaneous awareness of all places and of all beings. God's presence is formless, but it is a presence that is felt all the same. We don't see it but we can sense it. According to *Tao Te Ching*, a sacred text of Taoism:

> Look, it cannot be seen—it is beyond form.
> Listen, it cannot be heard—it is beyond sound.
> Grasp, it cannot be held—it is intangible.
> These three are indefinable;
> Therefore they are joined in one.[1]

This divine attribute of formlessness should remind us of our own formlessness. We are not solid bodies as we appear to be; we are composed of millions of atoms and molecules that move around and evolve within us. Another dimension of our formlessness is our soul that we can't see or touch, but which survives our physical body. Our timelessness is a dimension of our formlessness.

---

1.   Lao Tsu, *Tao Te Ching: A New Translation by Gia-Fu Feng and Jane English* (New York: Vintage Books, 1972), p. 14.

Never Ever Forgetting God

Sinful conduct can manifest itself in several ways. The greatest sin of all, according to Guru Nanak, is to forget God; to fail to remember that we live in a world that God made for us. The denial of our divinity is, therefore, the biggest sin. Who are those people who forget God? They are generally those who are so consumed by their success in life that they can't remember their own creator. There are many ups and downs in life. We do remember God in times of need. But if we are true to ourselves, if we are aware of the mystery that surrounds us in the form of this universe about which we have no clue, if we are conscious of our mortality, we will never forget the Supreme Being who gave us the most precious gift of all—the breath of life.

The Koran says ' ... remembrance of Allah is the greatest (thing in life) without doubt' (verse 29:45). God is the answer as well as the question. The solution requires contemplation. The problem is the eternal mystery.

Creation and Evolution

The Guru's creation mythology complements his conception of a formless God. He suggests an identifiable moment of creation, when a tremendous burst of energy started the evolutionary process. This process involved the unique role of the Creator; creation is the most magnificent work of God. The Creator made the world out of many elements, infusing divine light into every particle including the human being. Humans, therefore, did not evolve from lower species. Only human beings are blessed to pursue the spiritual path because of the potential for divine consciousness given to them at the time of creation. It is the potential in all of us, the infusion of holy energy at the start of creation, that enables us to seek God. We can experience this excitement of nature when we are genuinely in tune with our soul. What happened billions of years ago in a physical dimension happens every day in our spiritual quest.

Does that mean that Guru Nanak does not believe in evolution? Creation and evolution, he preached, go together. Creation is about the dynamic particles that provide a concrete shape to reality. Evolution, as the Creator's work in progress, is an expression of divine will. It is also the spiritual highway that makes the journey of the soul to higher planes possible. As we come closer to the Supreme through successive stages of physical and spiritual evolution, the secrets of creation are slowly revealed to us. The Creator never stops creating. What is accomplished at the physical level is also replicated at the spiritual level.

We are Spiritually Evolving Beings

This universe is an extraordinary creation of God. It is boundless in material possessions and boundless in its geographic expanse. There is no visible end to the planets, solar systems, and galaxies. Even the best of science can't keep track of the number because, with every scientific advance, discoveries of newer galaxies are produced. The secret of creation, as Guru Nanak reminds us, is the biggest mystery of all, and is known only to its Creator. We should respect this mystery and refrain from making unfounded claims.

How was this universe created? There are creation myths in many cultures that say that God, or a power subordinate to God, created this universe, which emerged only in response to the wishes of the Creator. Another view (considered a scientific perspective) holds that this world is the result of a long evolutionary process spread over five billion years. Human beings, animals, and plants have evolved from the first chemical substances through means of diversification and modification. Although the human offspring inherits a resemblance to their parents, they are not identical. Evolution, according to the Darwinian interpretation, proceeds by natural selection of well-adapted individuals through several centuries. Genetic changes primarily drive it. According to the most recent research, species tend to remain stable over long periods and then change abruptly. Apparently, these two views are incompatible. Many people see a conflict here. The world could not be a creation of God and also an object that is evolving on its own. To a logical mind, this does not appear convincing. However, in reality, creation and evolution are not either/or propositions.

Creation is a religious or spiritual idea. Evolution is a human discovery. Guru Nanak resolves the conflict between these positions. This universe is an act of creation, that is, a creation by a loving and caring God. But this creation is also the starting point of an evolutionary process that has gone on for millions of years. An evolution that unfolds the will of God in ways that are difficult for us to comprehend. In the following composition, Guru Nanak develops the theme of transition from physical creation to spiritual evolution. The physical world was created and left to evolve from the interplay of natural forces. But the human world, with the human body at its centre, was built with divine consciousness lodged at the pinnacle of human consciousness. Therefore, as human beings evolve spiritually, reaching upward to the highest levels of consciousness, they evolve from the lowest level of physical creation to the highest level of super consciousness. That is how a simple being becomes an enlightened being. The underlying process is nothing other than spiritual evolution.

> For countless years, there was nothing except darkness; there was
>   no earth, no heaven, only the Will of God.
> There was no day or night, no sun or moon;
> and the Creator was absorbed in deep meditation.
>
> There was no creation, no sound, no wind, no water.
> There was no being or non-being or transition from one to
>   the other.
> There were no regions, no seas, no rivers or flowing waters.
>
> There was no heaven, the mortal world, or lower region; neither hell
>   nor heaven nor time that perished the living.
> Concepts of hell and heaven, birth and death, were yet unknown.

There were no Brahma, Vishnu, or Shiva; only One Sole Presence was felt.
There were no male or female, caste, or birth.
There was no suffering, no joy.

There was no saint, no benevolent soul, no forest dweller; there were
      no fully formed, toiling, or lazy beings.
There was no yogi, no fully realized person.

There was no meditation, no austerity.
And no one talked of not this, not this [duality].
The Supreme created and valued Itself.

There was no initiation, no rosary for prayer.
There were no gopis, no Krishna, no cows or cowboys.
There was no magic, no spells, trickery, or soothing music.

There were no preferred actions, religions, or wealth attachments.
No one noticed one's caste at birth.
There were no attachments, no fears of death, no need to meditate.

There was no shame, no soul, no life.
There were no saints, no godlings.
There was no divine knowledge, no account of creation.

There was no higher or lower caste.
There was no god, no temple, no invocation.
There were no offerings, no fasts, no worships.

There was no scholar or judge.
There was no preacher, no one atoning, no pilgrimage.
There was no ruler, no subject, no high-sounding name.

There was no love, no devotion, no mind, no matter.
There was no friend or blood relation.
The Supreme, at Its pleasure, became a banker or a merchant.

There were no denominational books to read.
No prayers for sunrise or sunset.

The Supreme was the speaker who saw everything.

The world was created for His pleasure.
And without any support, the creation was sustained.
Brahma, Vishnu, and Shiva were created, and the love of the
    material world.

To a chosen few, God gave the Word.
The Supreme watched Its creation with loving care.
Within continents, solar systems, and lower regions,
the Supreme manifested Itself.

The Creator remained unattached but carved the human body as
    the most sacred centre of the universe.
The body was created combining elements of air, water, and fire.

The Creator created the nine zones of human consciousness;
and in the tenth zone divine energy was lodged—unknowable and
    limitless.
Seven seas of immaculate water were created to wash away dirt.

The lamps of sun and the moon were created to reflect divine light.
By creating them the Supreme celebrated Its own glory.
The Supreme became the source of honour and glory.

When blessings were received, death held no fear.
The devotee stood like a lotus flower in the water and remembered.

With the Supreme's command, the sky is opened.
With the Supreme's blessings, life abounds under, over, and above
    the earth.
With the Supreme's blessings, we breathe and sustain ourselves.

                                       [Raga Maru][1]

As Guru Nanak's composition reveals, evolution occurs on two levels: the physical level, which is easily measurable, and the spiritual level, which is unseen. Spiritual growth symbolizes the advancement of our individual and collective consciousness.

---

1   The author acknowledges the contribution of an unknown translator who translated these two hymns written in Raga Maru.

Leading a Virtuous Life

Guru Nanak divides our spiritual path, as mentioned earlier, into five distinct stages: moral living and rightful actions, search for divine knowledge, spiritual unfoldment, divine grace, and the final entry into the realm of Eternal Truth. Each stage is unique and vital. These stages appear as part of a sequence, and it is not possible for us to bypass any of these steps. For example, moral living is a precondition for the search of divine knowledge. A person who leads a morally decadent life will inevitably see no need to search for experiences of any kind, let alone spiritual knowledge. Also, our spirit cannot unfold unless we have accumulated sufficient spiritual energy during the first two stages. Any movement from this point onward is possible only when we receive divine grace, which is not our right but a 'reward' for good deeds. Leading a virtuous life is the very foundation of our spiritual quest. To go any further on the spiritual path, we need to make truthful and moral living an essential part of our life. It is only through such living that we make ourselves worthy of God's compassion and grace.

Growing up in a world where money can buy more comforts than it was possible at any other time in human history, how can we agree on a set of values and behaviours that would provide a reliable guide to a virtuous life? We need to acknowledge that there are some things which are moral, ethical, doable, and right under any circumstances. We may have a difference of opinion on whether it is moral to charge interest. But there should be no controversy on things like violence, falsehood, and exploitation of the poor and helpless. We need to identify some core values based on themes that cut across societal and cultural boundaries. The seven core values, based on Guru Nanak's teachings, are:

Non-violence Avoiding violence that hurts the innocent, kills, or insults (in the form of rape or other degrading actions) the victim, mass killings of innocent people in a war or a political conflict.

Truth Letting reality appear in its purest form, separating facts from opinions, not using falsehood of any kind to deceive other people, treating honest living as a sacred obligation.

Love Showing sympathy and compassion for a victim of oppression, having a sense of justice, keeping a charitable spirit, sharing one's wealth and good fortune with the poor and the needy.

Virtue The pursuit of highest personal morality in one's daily life, respecting the honour and integrity of one's partner, taking responsibility for one's children, catering to their material, emotional, and intellectual needs, caring for the needs of elders in the family.

Communitarianism Being a good citizen, participating in electoral processes, raising voice against misdeeds of those in authority, using public office for public good, protecting the natural environment, giving one's employer a fair share of one's time, talent, and ability.

Equality Treating all people as equal despite differences of colour, race, gender, or ethnic origins, respecting cultural and spiritual traditions of other people.

Theism Having faith in the unbounded love, mercy, and compassion of the Creator for all things and all beings.

It is not an attempt to define a new morality. It has not been easy for moral philosophers, who have struggled with these issues over the ages.

We can look at various opinions, or what our belief system has to say about these matters, but, in the end, we need to have an objective look at how we are coping with difficult moral and ethical choices in our life. This freedom for self-evaluation is not a blank cheque, meaning whatever serves our needs or purposes is acceptable. We need to cultivate, in the words of Albert Einstein, a moral attitude in and towards life based on the totality of our being—body, mind, and soul. Not doing this self-evaluation in a seriously mindful way would indicate our reluctance to follow a spiritual path.

Caring for Others and Showing Compassion

Guru Nanak celebrates the unity of people who love and worship God. Believers are encouraged to spend time together (*sangat*) in sharing their blessings and sorrows and eating food together while reciting the Name. This sense of belonging and spiritual bonding is the nourishment they need to expand their reach into the unknown. Therefore, we have to be caring and compassionate human beings.

Guru Arjan Dev, the fifth Sikh guru, explains the reason for all believers to have a sense of belonging. We are residents, he says, of the city founded by God. The founder is the source of all blessings and joys. It is only in being together that our objectives are fulfilled. When people are together, they do not cause pain or injury to one another. When peace comes to a small number of people, it gradually extends to all of humankind. And in peace and contemplation lies the path of self-realization.

Realizing that Actions Have Consequences

We may be condemned to repeat our journey or even regress in terms of our spiritual development. This is the lesson of karma or predestination. As we sow, so shall we reap, says Guru Nanak. This idea, known as the Golden Rule (do unto others as you would have them do unto you), appears in every major wisdom tradition in one form or another.

What happens when we don't live by the Golden Rule? We end up having karmic accumulation that is undesirable for the evolution of our soul. There is a way, says Guru Nanak, to combat this karmic cycle. Prayer, worship, meditation, moral living: all these modes of spiritual life will help us gain divine grace, which means that with our own effort we can reverse negative karmic energy into something positive. But if we continue to hurt other people and spend our entire life in material attachments, we can't hope to gain enlightenment. The forceful cycle of karma will continue to exact its toll.

God is omnipresent and omniscient. We cannot hide anything from the all-seeing eye of God. It watches all our actions. There is a precise measurement in the sense that the standard applied is fair, objective, and compassionate. In a way, this is the logical extension of the law of karma. Although this accounting is perfect, what we get in practice is determined by several factors, the most important of which is divine grace. We have to accept whatever comes our way. As Guru Nanak says:

Nanak, for human beings,
it is idle to ask for pleasure when suffering comes;

pleasure and suffering are robes that we must wear.
Where arguing is of no avail, it is best to be contented.

[Var Majh]

After we leave this world,

we are asked to give an account of our deeds,

which are already recorded in the divine register.

We can't escape or rebel against this.

We are caught in a blind alley and there is no place to go.

Says Nanak, destroy the falsehood

and let the truth prevail.

[Ramkali Ki Var]

Becoming Socially Responsive and a Catalyst for Positive Change

Our society, culture, and economic system are all part of the more significant order created for us by God. But at the micro level, subsystems are humanly designed and implemented and thus are imperfect and unjust in several ways. Only divine order is perfect and just. If we accept and submit ourselves to the divine law, we can bring perfection to our social and economic institutions. It is, therefore, important to acknowledge that 'in God we trust' is a required affirmation to live in the kingdom of God and to establish the supremacy of an order based on superordinate values. A society that does not trust in God manifests as tyranny and, thus, disintegrates under the weight of its own contradictions.

Guru Nanak advocates rule of law and exercise of power by the collective will of the people. He says:

The ruler who submits to democratic ideals,
his rule is lasting.

[Raga Maru]

Therefore, democracy is not merely a human innovation; it is a reflection of the will of God—something borrowed by us from the divine order that the Creator had in mind for us. Given this, all dictatorial regimes are violations of the divine order. They crush the human spirit, making the journey of the soul more hazardous and tortuous. A free society, where people have a voice and freedom to practice their religion and spiritual values, is heaven on earth. Corrupt and oppressive regimes are reflective of hell and are a domain of Satan.

As we relinquish ourselves to the loving care of God, we release spiritual energy that can work for us and promote the common good. This energy has a great 'healing touch', not only for individual ailments but for social pathologies such as crime, poverty, and social alienation. Spiritual life, in practice, is a life devoted to the well-being of the community. Spiritual growth and communal life go hand in hand.

God-centred people, according to Guru Nanak, are not self-centred. They think of themselves as a small part of the much more significant social organism. This harmony between the individual and the community occurs spontaneously, without any personal effort. Selfishly living for oneself is a very narrow attitude given all the possibilities that life has to offer. Once we become role models for others, we start to radiate our spiritual energy to benefit those around us. That is why *Japji* says that devotees, men and women who genuinely believe in God, not only immortalize themselves but also help their loved ones—friends, family members, and associates— manage the difficult transition from the material to the spiritual life and even beyond to the immortal life.

A spiritual life following the divine order can have a significant effect on our inner and outer existence. There is no real separation between body and soul. We need to take care of our physical body to provide a suitable environment for our soul to gain its unfoldment. Guru Nanak attaches great importance to personal cleanliness, proper nourishment, outdoor activities, and community service.

The Personal Sense of Right and Wrong

We need to nurture and develop our ethics to guide our values and behaviours. Personal ethics may be drawn from our religious convictions or our moral temperament, which we owe to our parents or spiritual mentors. It is not a one-time effort. It is the job of a lifetime. We need to reinforce our values through the use of appropriate myths, metaphors, rituals, or whatever other avenues for spiritual development are available to us.

Religious orthodoxy in India takes the view that a variety of ritualistic actions can cleanse the evil we do in this life. Guru Nanak is opposed to such acts as they do not add any spiritual value. It is only through total inner transformation and not through the performance of outward actions that we realize God. Whether rituals are good or bad is not an easy question to settle. Possibly, there are beneficial rituals that can add richness and variety to our spiritual life. But we have to be careful about how we define the term. If the ritual is acting with one's free will, with the conscious understanding that it would add worth to one's life, then there is no harm in performing that action. For example, all actions performed by choice, such as reading from a particular scripture at an appointed hour, or pursuits of daily life such as taking a walk, writing a journal, or playing a musical instrument are all healthy and provide nourishment to our soul in addition to enhancing our commitment to a values-driven life. The critical test is whether rituals are facilitating our inner transformation, or are they symbols of outward life, without any direct connection to our 'soul work'.

Environment as Our Spiritual Guide and Companion

Environment or nature is the most beautiful part of our planet. We assume that in other worlds, there are natural systems that may be even more beautiful. Nature is the imagination and the work of a supreme artist. There is, therefore, something sacred about nature that must be acknowledged. Caring for the preservation of nature as God's creation, according to Guru Nanak, is a requirement as well as a vehicle for our spiritual advancement.

If the connection between nature and God is real, it follows that nature has sanctity far beyond the economic rationale of being merely a 'natural resource' that is available to us for our comfort and profit. We should become custodians of this resource instead of being silent spectators of its ruthless exploitation and destruction. We should indeed make it our spiritual guide and companion.

Nature is the cradle of great cultural and spiritual traditions, especially of indigenous peoples around the world. Nature is our accompaniment in the process of gaining enlightenment. Buddha gained enlightenment under a tree. The Himalayas were traditionally the home of rishis in the ancient Vedic period. God spoke to Moses from inside a burning bush. Forests in Eastern and Western mythologies are a place of wonder and amusement. As mythologist Joseph Campbell used to say, the hero in his search for spiritual fulfilment never enters the forest where there is a well-trodden path. Like the spirit, the forest hides what it has in store for us. However, it never disappoints.[1]

---

1   Joseph Campbell, *The Hero With a Thousand Faces* (New York: Pantheon Books, 1949).

Many religious scriptures, including the Bible and the Koran, describe in vivid detail our connection with the earth, air, sky, and water. The changing colours of nature, including the change of seasons, represent our changing moods, periods of our moral and spiritual growth, and the uniqueness of our personalities. Nature is our connection with the rest of the universe. When we look at the forest, we can see the sky beyond it, and we can look at the stars, galaxies, and the whole dance of the universe. Nature has a spiritual and cultural dimension, but it is also a practical asset for the preservation of the human race due to the many useful functions performed by it.

If nature is so critical for our survival as a species, how can we strengthen our bonds with it? There are many practical suggestions from the literature that has come to be known as 'deep ecology'. Here are a few useful things we can do: understand the way nature works; understand the natural harmony that exists between individuals, communities, and the environment; simplify wants and cut down on the consumption of non-essentials; aim to meet only vital needs and recycle; help create decentralized, non-hierarchical, and democratic systems and structures; recognize that nature has intrinsic worth; remember that a species once extinct is gone forever; and that when we destroy our environment, we destroy ourselves.

Monitoring Our Spiritual Progress

The length of time lived, measured in months and years, is not as important as the quality of life itself, particularly the spiritual content. Do we spend our life doing good? Do we remember God? Do we spend time in meditation? Our faith (higher moral values and commitments, and a strong belief system) can play an essential role in keeping us robust to fight repression and injustice, help us withstand various temptations, and even make sacrifices for worthy causes.

When we decide to lead a spiritual life, it causes us to look differently at our priorities. How do we spend our time? What are the things that are most essential to us? It is, therefore, important to keep track of our spiritual progress. Guru Nanak asks us to pay attention to our preferred way of life:

Our nights are spent sleeping,
our days in pursuit of physical needs.
This life,
which is as precious as a jewel goes for a seashell.
What an act of foolishness!
If we don't spend our time in God realization,
we will regret a lot in the end.

[Gauri Bairagan]

Realization of Truth is higher than all else;
higher still is truthful living.

[Sri Raga Ashtpadi]

Poetry and Music as Tools
for Spiritual Progress

Poetry and music are essential in many sacred traditions. They are more so in the spiritual tradition established by Guru Nanak. Although *Japji* is not supposed to be sung (it is meant to be read slowly), several other compositions of Guru Nanak were written for specific ragas in the Indian classical tradition. All compositions in the *Sri Guru Granth Sahib* are written in verse and, wherever a raga is specified, are supposed to be sung in the prescribed raga. The Guru's fondness for music is evident in several passages. Music is a divine craft suitable for gods and goddesses, and poetry is the medium through which the soul expresses itself.

Spiritual philosopher Thomas Moore writes: 'We know ... from countless paintings of angels that there is a music that is truly heavenly, not of this world. Or could it be that music and soul-stirring sounds link our daily life to eternal things? Ficino said that music comes to us on air that has been tempered by sound, sets in motion the air spirit of the person, and then affects the heart and penetrates to the most intimate levels of the mind. And this music is directly tied to the music of the world, its rhythms, and modalities.'[1]

---

1 Thomas Moore, *The Re-Enchantment of Everyday Life* (New York: HarperCollins, 1996), p. 111.

Conquering Our Ego-Mind

What is ego? Sri Ramakrishna once used an analogy to clarify the distinction between ego and soul. He gave the example of an old-style horse carriage. The person sitting above the horses and driving the wagon is our ego-mind. The person who is inside the carriage is our soul—the real owner. As long as ego is doing the driving, we go here and there without any sense of direction, trying to control everything that comes our way. But when our soul is awakened and takes control, we find our true destination.

People with strong egos have an inflated view of their physical and mental capacities. They love to demean other people and their potential, and they display all kinds of bad behaviour in their interactions with others. Conquering the ego-mind, according to Guru Nanak, is the biggest battle for all human beings. Once we can subdue our controlling tendencies, we start to look upon life differently. Flow comes back into our lives. We open our mind to new ideas, new possibilities. The door to our transformation is opened and we become more loving, more compassionate, and more sensitive. But this door to self-transformation can be opened only with strong self-determination.

Our ego-mind also breeds ignorance, creating wrong notions about ourselves and the world. We start to filter information. Such an attitude slows our mental and spiritual advancement. Ignorance, nourished by the ego-mind, can take many forms: we may be ignorant of our purpose in life and our relationship with God, or we commit acts of violence or injustice against others. People who rob, rape, terrorize, mutilate, or injure other people are ignorant of the consequences of their actions. Once we start nourishing our soul, and our soul starts feeding us and our ego slowly withers away, making our life fruitful for us and others.

Mental Balance, Tranquility, and Contentment

Mental balance, tranquility, and contentment are critical in a world full of choices and opportunities. If our happiness depends on the level of our material acquisitions, we would never reach a point where we would be fully satisfied. On the other hand, if we adopt contentment as a way of life, it would be unaffected by our daily gains and losses. We will have happiness in all stages of our life.

Honest effort is the only real effort that counts. With reasonable effort, we can move ahead, achieve our life goals, and be genuinely proud of our attainments. But some of us think that there are shortcuts; that we can move ahead quicker if we compromise our principles and our integrity; that what counts is the result and not the means. That is faulty logic. There is no choice between means and ends. We need the right outcomes using the right methods.

Self-restraint complements mental contentment and honest effort. People who can restrain their desires and impulses are more likely to be honest in their efforts and have greater peace of mind. The many choices and temptations offered by the consumer society in which we live make self-restraint a necessity. We need to centre our mind. Says Guru Nanak:

> The restless mind is not centred at one place;
> like a deer, it nibbles at tender shoots.
> If we were to lodge in our mind the divine lotus feet,
> we would live longer with an awakened mind.
> All human beings suffer from anxiety,
> but by the contemplation of God comes bliss.
>
> [Ramkali Dakhni Onkar]

When we are fully contented, we are touched by a presence that is much larger than our own life. The sacred touch, by necessity, is a tender touch. Tenderness and sensitivity thus become essential dimensions of our humanity. There can be no love without caring for others' feelings. People who are rude or disrespectful in their behaviour, who are insensitive to human suffering, have only one thing in common: they have shut love out of their lives to pursue other objectives. They seem to forget that when love goes out of their lives, not much is left.

We have a hidden treasure, Guru Nanak reminds us, inside all of us. However, most of the time we are unaware of what we are capable of achieving. Self-discovery of our real potential is not possible without getting in touch with our inner core. That is the function of meditation. It is only in pure silence, when all internal dialogue is suspended, that we start to discover who we are. It is through the process of finding our divinity that we find ourselves.

A Gift of Grace

In every heart shines the Eternal Light
which we discover with guru's direction.

[Sri Raga]

Divine grace is the central pillar of Guru Nanak's spirituality. It finds a prominent place in several meditations of *Japji* and in his hymns. If the Lord is not pleased, nothing will be gained. Grace is an essential condition that a devotee must fulfil to reach his or her ultimate goal in life. Personal transformation is possible at all times. All human beings can gain spiritually if they take the path of virtue and conquer their ego-mind. It is never too late. This goal is always within our reach.

Forever in love with created beings,
The Creator is a custodian of our well-being.
O Saviour, invaluable are Your blessings;
without any limit is Your power to bestow merit.

[Kirtan Sohila]

Human effort alone is not enough. There is a stage in our spiritual evolution where we do not progress any further without the gift of divine grace. Only when we are divinely blessed can we hope to climb different steps on the spiritual ladder and reach our goals.

This is the gift of grace
Listless foolish talk is all else.

[Sri Raga]

PART II
JAPJI SAHIB
MEDITATIONS

In many spiritual traditions, the sunrise is a sacred moment. It is the time of the day when nature wakes up from its nightly slumber. Birds sing, and the journey of life begins for another day. At a mythical level, there is a death and a rebirth. The night that dies becomes a part of our collective memory. The day that is born brings hope and joy. We are awakened to the mystery of life, our consciousness slowly spreads its wings, and we begin to savour the taste of life. What better time could we find to seek oneness with our Creator, whose love and care makes it possible for us to add yet another day to our lives!

> When dawn breaks,
> We sing glories of Your greatness. [4]

As morning prayer, *Japji Sahib* (from the word *jap* or *jaap*, meaning chanting, reciting, or meditating) is unique in many ways. This composition represents the very essence of Guru Nanak's spiritual and cosmological beliefs. It is the foundation of the Sikh (meaning 'disciple') faith. Consisting of a prologue, thirty-eight meditations, and an epilogue, *Japji Sahib* commends the path of unconditional love—a complete submission to the command of a loving God.

Japji Sahib is also the opening composition in the *Adi Granth*, the first scripture. The *granth* contains mystical writings of Sikh gurus and other revered saints such as Kabir. The fifth guru, Guru Arjan Dev, compiled it and it was later vested with the power and sanctity of a living guru and transformed into *Sri Guru Granth Sahib* by the tenth and last guru, Guru Gobind Singh, in 1708. The reverence shown to the *Sri Guru Granth Sahib* as a living embodiment of the supreme guru is unmatched by any other scripture.

Prologue
One True Supreme Being

Ek Onkaar Sat Naam
Kartaa Purakh
Nirbha-o Nirvair
Akaal Muurat
Ajuunii Saibhan
Gur Parsaad

One True Name,
the Creator,
without fear and hate;
Timeless Form,
Unborn,
Self-existent,
Self-illumined,
attainable only through Guru's grace!

Jap

Aad sach
Jugaad sach.
Hai bhee sach
Naanak hosee bhee sach

Meditate

One and True at the beginning
and in the primal age.

Who is True, says Nanak,
and shall ever remain True!

Japji Sahib begins with a prologue (*mool mantra*), which is a beautiful statement of Guru Nanak's fundamental belief about the nature of God (*Waheguru*) and our relationship with Him. 'One True Supreme Being' is a powerful affirmation of the unity of God. The specific qualities of God, such as truth, fearlessness, timelessness, and formlessness, which reinforce the concept of One God, are as follows.

Truth is equated with God as truth is the very essence of God. The human conception of truth is often tainted by our own limited vision of what is right or wrong. Therefore, truth is something relative to our existence and our experiences. We are unable to see the ultimate truth or the eternal order that God has created for us. The eternal truth is beyond our imagination and understanding. For God, there is no duality, because in God's presence, everything manifests itself as unity. Everything unfolds its true nature; there is no possibility of any false appearance as God sees the true essence of everything. There are no half-truths in this realm—either something exists in its true essence or not at all. There is nothing that is relative in the sense of being true, subject to the existence of other causal factors. In the divine presence, there is no other causality.

God is beyond all fear. Fear is the product of our ego-mind and our dependence on the external world. Spiritual energy, being pure consciousness, is above ego. We are unable to see the inner reality in view of our enslavement by our ego-mind. The ego creates fear because it also creates attachments. When we are attached to other people and things, we have to learn to live with the fear of losing them. This creates insecurity, which in turn leads to more fear, including the biggest fear of all—the fear of dying.

God is above malice, which is a human tendency born in the absence of love. If we completely fill ourselves with love and develop the strength to practice love as the sole principle of living, we can get rid of hate. People who immerse their identities in the divine name are free from all fears and feelings of hate.

God is loving and merciful. Creation is the work of God's love and compassion. We have been given a rare opportunity to participate in the wonders of this magical universe. The creation is so vast and so varied that the Creator can't be anything but a fountain of love and compassion for all living beings. We would not be able to live without fresh air that rejuvenates us at all times. We would not be able to quench our thirst without fresh, clean water. We would have nothing to eat without fertile soil. The merciful and loving God provided this for us and we need to preserve this gift of love. In reality, human beings have not been very good custodians and caretakers. We have filled the air with noxious fumes. We have polluted the rivers and streams with toxic substances. We have burned and destroyed forests. We have denuded the soil of its nutrients. And we continue to indulge in acts of destruction and vandalism that harm the global environment. We do it because we have forgotten that these natural assets are God's creation and gift.

God is formless and timeless. We are able to identify ourselves easily with a personal God. We assume that He has the same appearance as a human being. It is difficult, however, to picture a formless God—a presence without an appearance. Yet, it is important to understand that God's visible manifestation cannot be limited to a form and shape that belongs only to the human race, which is but one among several billion species created by God.

The idea of formlessness cannot be separated from the idea of timelessness. Anything that is limited to a given form cannot be timeless. Guru Nanak presents a conception of God that modern science, in particular quantum physics, has uncovered only in this century.

Everything we see or touch is made up of matter that can be reduced to subatomic particles. This division follows an endless rhythm; its ultimate limits have not been reached by even the most advanced science. Based on what we know, it is clear that the tiniest particles move in an empty space, which in relative terms is equal to the distance of one galaxy from another. Within this visible body of ours, there is an empty space that cannot be measured in precise terms, even with the most sophisticated scientific instruments. Yet, all of us are unaware of our own formlessness.

The formless God is the energy that powers everything—meteors, glaciers, tropical forests, animals, human beings et al. God, as a subtle form of energy, is present in everything and everywhere. Places of worship are convenient sites for us to get in touch with God, but there is no place and no being that is untouched by God's love at any time. In order for us to experience this presence, we have to develop our capacity to see something that we do not ordinarily see, and to hear the voice that is not normally audible to our ears. What we do not see is the presence of a formless God, and the voice that we do not hear, in fact, is the divine melody hidden in the depths of our hearts.

God is un-incarnate, self-existent, self-generating, and immortal. Humans have none of these attributes. Our mortality is predetermined. Our life is like a journey of self-realization, of finding meaning in what we are, and using the power of the Name to attain a state of bliss after this life—our union with a loving God. The Creator has no need to go through the process of living and dying. The Supreme was present before creation and will be there long after the creation has ceased to be. God is not limited by this world as we know it. God's worlds and realms are beyond our reckoning. Death is a requirement for us; it is, in reality, a ladder for our enlightenment. Living this life is essential for us because it is only during this life that our soul gets the opportunity to express itself, to explore its potential, and to find a direction beyond the reach of this life.

God is also the supreme preceptor; the greatest spiritual guide, mentor, and teacher of all. This is the manifest form of God. But this manifestation does not take the form of an avatar, a God in visible form. God is an inner experience open to all human beings, irrespective of their status in life. Preceptor, in this sense, is the holy word that helps us attain our spiritual goals.

The word 'meditate' (*jap*), at the start of *Japji Sahib*, lends itself to more than one interpretation. First, it suggests a title for this whole set of meditations. Second, it is a command to recite the Name and to immerse oneself in the meditations that follow. Third, it helps us to get into a genuinely meditative mood. *Japji Sahib*, in its essence, is an invitation to honour, celebrate, recite, and internalize this creation, and, through this celebration, advance the momentum of our own spiritual evolution.

We are reminded of God's existence when time was not measured in the way we measure it now. Our concept of time starts with the Big Bang, the starting point for planetary evolution, and it will end with the Big Crunch, the starting point for the universe to commence material contraction. God has lived through the known as well as unknown segments of geologic time, and will continue to live beyond this visible reality. This means that God is beyond time, and the divine presence in this universe transcends any quantitative measurement known to us.

Intellectual or meditative pursuits are necessary but not sufficient conditions to unravel the great mystery of our being and our relationship with God. The material world is inadequate to satisfy our spiritual cravings. Rational thinking is equally deficient. We need to realize that we are governed by the divine order, which is an expression of the will of God. This is not a scientific puzzle or a clever gimmick. Everything is divinely ordained. Nothing happens by chance. By submitting our will to the will of God, we enlarge the expanse of our awareness—an awareness that brings us true freedom.

1
The Divine Order

Sochai soch na hova-ii jay sochii lakh vaar.
Chupai chup na hova-ii jay laa-ay rahaa liv taar.
Bhukhi-aa bhukh na utrii jay bannaa purii-aa bhaar.
Sahas si-aanpaa lakh hohi ta ik na chalai naal.
Kiv sachi-aaraa ho-ii-ai kiv koorhai tutai paal.
Hukam rajaa-ee chalnaa Naanak likhi-aa naal.

We cannot get to know Him through monotonous thinking.
Real silence is not attained through trance-like meditation.
Neither through worldly possessions is this hunger appeased,
nor through a million other mental feats is enlightenment achieved.
How to prove our truth before Him and lift the veil of darkness?
Only submission to the divine order, which is preordained,
says Nanak, can get us awareness!

In this meditation, we are introduced to the concept of the divine order, which is not just a spiritual or philosophical concept. It is the reality that we face every day. Look at the working of nature—sunrise, sunset, change of seasons, and the rotation of the earth around the sun. There is order; there is a hidden pattern. All these natural phenomena are part of the divine order. What is the supreme power behind all this disposition? We do not even have the mental capacity to assess the might of that entity. We may harbour illusions about our own physical and spiritual powers; we think we can attain great things through our efforts. In reality, what we need is the realization that whatever we seek is within our grasp as long as our actions align with the divine order.

Only through the process of this realization can we ensure that the results we seek will come our way. No clever schemes or devices will work. What is needed is an acceptance of the fact that the divine order and its creator are the final and only arbiters of our destiny.

We have to give unconditional love to obtain unconditional love from the Lord. Seeking material things makes for conditional love. The veil of darkness that surrounds us symbolizes the ignorance of our position on this planet, not knowing where we come from and where we go. Once this veil is lifted, a glow of divine love suddenly illuminates our life. Then we can see ourselves as spiritual beings and understand how the entirety of existence is divinely guided. Our journey is not a chance happening. It is the continuation of our yearning to lead a life of eternal bliss. This awareness should bring us closer to our true freedom—the freedom to realize the fullest potential of our soul-being.

2

The Divine Order and Divine Grace

Hukmii hovan aakaar hukam na kahi-aa jaa-ii.
Hukmii hovan jii-a hukam milai vadi-aa-ii.
Hukmii utam niich hukam likh dukh sukh paa-ii-ah.
Iknaa hukmii bakhsiis ik hukmii sadaa bhavaa-ii-ah.
Hukmai andar sabh ko baahar hukam na ko-ay.
Naanak hukmai jay bujhai ta ha-umai kahai na ko-ay.

The divine order that creates life is not easy to name.
It gives life and confers honour and fame.
It makes us high or low, happy or sad.
His grace saves some, others live and are born again.
The divine order encompasses and rules us all.
Believers, says Nanak, have no ego-mind at all!

This meditation is a celebration of the divine order and grace. Whatever experiences we have in life—happiness, joy, sorrow—are the gradual unfoldment of the order that supersedes everything else. From the pain of the separation to the bliss of the union, these are gifts that our Creator has assembled for us. We should live and enjoy every moment. The fire that burns inside us is our prayer, our meditation. Not even for a moment should we be blindly driven by our ego-mind. Our existence itself is a glorious and generous act of our Creator.

As controller of this universe, God makes it possible for various life forms or species to be born. The enormous variety of animals, birds, fish, and plants, known as biodiversity, is a testimony to the limitless imagination of the maker to conceive such myriad forms and infuse them with the gift of life. Such an artist is beyond expression in words. We can imagine the utter sublimity and grandeur of God but are unable to ascribe meaning to this scheme of things.

All honours and rewards can be traced back to the divine order. That is why it is important to remember that truly blessed are those who live with the full realization of the absolute authority of God. This thought is central to their very existence; not even for a second do they forget their need to totally submit to the dictates of God. Lest it sounds somewhat authoritarian, we need to remember that God is not a despot. God is the source of all caring and nurturing. By submitting ourselves to God's command, we submit ourselves to the constant flow of love that fills our body and soul with grace, compassion, unity, and immortality.

Quite often, we take pride in our worldly achievements. But the real achievement comes with divine grace. Our life is a roller coaster of highs and lows, with moments of happiness and sadness. We should not be too happy when we are at a peak, and we should not be too disheartened when we hit the ground. We need to remember that everything that happens to us has a divine purpose. If we lead a life of prayer and meditation, there is nothing for us to worry about. In the midst of happiness or pain, we can enjoy moments of bliss, provided we continue to follow the right path. Our life is painful because it is part of the eternal life-and-death cycle. Our birth is a traumatic event. Our life is full of pain and suffering because we never fully achieve what we want. In the end, we lose what is precious to us: positions of power and authority, comforts and riches, friends and relatives. In every dark alley in our life, there is the shadow of death; the fear of being crippled and incapacitated. The only way for us to get out of this cycle of life and death is to seek atonement, to elevate our life to a higher plane of consciousness where we conquer our ego and submerge our identity in the ocean of love that surrounds us, but whose presence we tend to ignore.

The divine order extends to all beings without any exception. The powerful among us entertain illusions of immortality, thinking that they can use deceit and cunning. By the time they realize their folly, it is generally too late. Worldly possessions and vestiges of worldly power stay behind us; we move forward on our eternal journey only with our good deeds. The Guru warns us that we must shed our false pride and self-centredness and submit ourselves to the divine order if we seek salvation from the cycle of pain and suffering.

3

Many Dimensions of Divine Love

Gaavai ko taan hovai kisai taan.
Gaavai ko daat jaanai niisaan.
Gaavai ko gun vadi-aa-ii-aa chaar.
Gaavai ko vidi-aa vikham viichaar.
Gaavai ko saaj karay tan khayh.
Gaavai ko jii-a lai fir dayh.
Gaavai ko jaapai disai door.
Gaavai ko vaykhai haadraa haduur.
Kathnaa kathii na aavai tot.
Kath kath kathii kotii kot kot.
Daydaa day laiday thak paahi.
Jugaa jugantar khaahii khaahi.
Hukmii hukam chalaa-ay raahu.
Naanak vigsai vayparvaahu.

Some praise His might.
Some praise His generosity.
Some praise His virtue and knowledge.
Some praise His ability to create and destroy.
Some praise His gift of renewal and regeneration.
Some praise His detachment and distance.
Some praise His omnipresence and attention.
There is no end to our praise and our description;
millions have showered upon Him praises and veneration.
He gives us untiringly, but the recipients get wearied;
through the ages, we have lived on His benediction.

The movement of this universe is divinely willed.

There is joy and rejoicing, says Nanak, in His giving!

There are many ways to praise God. People look at one facet and get carried away. In reality, there are countless dimensions of the Lord, with no inherent contradictions. If we open our eyes with love, we shall see the most beautiful vision—always generous, encouraging, forgiving, and nudging us to move forward. We should accept the totality of this vision, submitting ourselves to the will of the Creator.

This meditation presents different human perceptions of God. Some people are impressed by the power at God's command. For them, God is the source of immense might with the power to create and to destroy. This perception results in fear. Other people look upon God as the source of all knowledge and learning. Some are swayed by God's life-giving and life-destroying attributes. There are those who think that God is very detached, far removed from the rough and tumble of their daily lives. And there are those, although a small minority, who think that they are never bereft of divine love and compassion.

Although it might appear paradoxical, God is all these things and more. Human imagination can never find limits to divine manifestations. There are no limits to God's generosity. God controls a treasury of gifts that are far beyond our imagination. We can get tired of receiving an endless chain of gifts, but the Creator knows no end to the care and nurture of this vast creation of which we are an integral part.

There is freedom to choose our relationship with the Supreme based on our own preferences: like a mighty force, a benevolent being, a source of wisdom, or a creator and destroyer of life. But we have no freedom to ignore the fact that the divine order will prevail under all circumstances. It is only through this realization that we can find meaning and purpose in our life.

4

The Pristine Love of the Supreme Beloved

Saachaa saahib saach naa-ay bhaakhi-aa bhaa-o apaar.
Aakhahe mangahe dayhei dayhei daat karay daataar.
Fayr ke agai rakhii-ai jit disai darbaar.
Muhou ke bolan bolii-ai jit sun dharay pi-aar.
Amrit vaylaa sach naa-o vadi-aa-ii viichaar.
Karmii aavai kaprhaa nadrii mokh du-aar.
Naanak ayvai jaanii-ai sabh aapay sachiaar.

He, who is eternal and just, speaks in the language of love.
We ask for gifts and receive endless benediction.
What can we offer in return?
What prayer can we offer to receive His love which is pristine?
When dawn breaks, we sing glories of His greatness.
We gain human body as a gift of compassion
and the door to liberation is opened by His merciful glance.
To know the True One, says Nanak, is to know the Supreme Lord.

The embodiment of truth speaks to us in the language of love. As human beings, we have some understanding of love and its manifestations, but divine love is much deeper and sweeter than the love we experience in our daily lives. The rain shower of the Lord's love, when experienced, is the ultimate joy of peace, compassion, beauty, and bliss at the same time. It is love that accepts no boundaries. Bounded love is a typical human fallacy, dependent on other conditions that are satisfied by its recipients. Divine love knows no beginning or end. Once we receive it, it will stay with us forever. Our path will shine, and our journey beyond this life will be smooth on the pathway that connects life with death.

Once we realize that God is a generous giver of valuable gifts, we may raise our demands. We can ask for things of material value. We can ask for gifts of happiness for ourselves and for those whom we love. We may want things to happen here and now. This is not a problem. For the generous dispenser of love and happiness, no demand is too big. But the question is, how do we repay our debt? Material offerings could only have symbolic meaning because matter has no permanent value other than being a speck in the cosmic dust. The way to fulfil our obligations is to open our hearts and minds to the Lord's presence. We should, therefore, engross ourselves in the meditation of the Name.

It is known that our birth in this life is determined by our past actions or karma. Karma, or predestination, is the law of dynamic causation and interaction between the higher and lower levels of our being. As the soul goes through a variety of experiences, we can reach a higher level if our actions in this life so warrant. In the soul's journey through time, we can accumulate rewards for good deeds. In the same way, our wrongdoings can pull us down in our evolutionary path. As long as our lower nature remains active, we continue to incur karmic deeds. But this is not simple causation, nor is it a simple game of chance.

This meditation combines karmic results with the most important need for grace. When everything is counted, our liberation from the cycle of life and death depends on divine grace. Good actions alone are not sufficient. They can pave the way, but unless we fill our lives with the love of God and submit ourselves to the divine order, there can be no release and enlightenment.

5

He Transcends All Material Manifestations

Thaapi-aa na jaa-ay kiitaa na ho-ay.
Aapay aap niranjan so-ay.
Jin sayvi-aa tin paa-i-aa maan.
Naanak gaavii-ai gunee nidhaan.
Gaavii-ai sunii-ai man rakhii-ai bhaa-o.
Dukh parhar sukh ghar lai jaa-ay.
Gurmukh naada gurmukh vaydan gurmukh rahi-aa samaa-ii.
Gur iisar gur gorakh barmaa gur paarbatii maa-ii.
Jay ha-o jaanaa aakhaa naahii kahnaa kathan na jaa-ii.
Guraa ik dayhei bujhaa-ii.
Sabhnaa jii-aa kaa ik daataa so mai visar na jaa-ii.

Neither seen in physical form nor created in any manner,
He is immaculate and self-existent.
Those who serve the True One are profoundly meritorious.
Nanak sing praises of the treasure of virtue!
Sing and hear the glories of the Lord!
He takes away misery and gives fulfilment.
The sound of the sacred word is divine knowledge,
and the word itself is all-pervasive and resplendent.
God is Shiva, Vishnu, and Brahma;
Goddess is Parvati, Lakshmi, and Sarasvati.
Even if I understand the True One, I cannot put it in words.
I simply pray for enlightenment.
Guru gave me one advice: there is one God of all creation,
let me not forget.

This meditation reminds us of God's true nature. Being formless, shapeless, and self-creating, God is free from constraints that bind us and limit our potential as human beings. We have a form that we inherit at birth. We are self-creating only in a limited sense. We can grow only within the boundaries of our potential. God is beyond any limitations and truly self-generating in the sense of transcending all material manifestations.

Meditation of the Name is not only an obligation but also an honour. Blessed are the souls who are so evolved that they are able to recite the Name. Lowly creatures and human beings at the lower end of their spiritual evolution are not so blessed. They are unaware of the pleasure that is available to those who recite the Name. True devotees are unaffected by the pangs of sorrow that can break the spirit of ordinary folks. They not only experience happiness on their own but also spread it around. Imagine the effect the presence of a god-loving person has on his or her environment. Rays of light seem to emanate from the pores of such a person. The air gets lighter and fragrant. Good thoughts fill the air with their intensity and depth of meaning. Hatred, malice, selfishness, and other negative energies evaporate into thin air. This is the magic of divine love.

When we carry a divine aura or meet someone who is divinely blessed, we experience a sudden change in our surroundings. This is why people recite holy prayers at the time of sickness or death of their dear ones. When the Name is uttered, no evil spirit can stay around. Eternal peace prevails. The pain of sickness can be reduced or totally eliminated. The path of the dying person can thus be cleared.

This meditation refers to the trinity of gods: Brahma, Vishnu, and Shiva. Shiva is the destroyer (destruction being a stage in the process of creation), and, in many respects, a god of gods (Mahadeva). Vishnu is the preserver and, in this role, is the embodiment of the qualities of mercy and goodness. Brahma is the creator of the universe, the God of wisdom, and the guardian of the Vedas. Parvati, Shiva's consort and female energy, is Mother Durga, who, in another incarnation, destroys Mahesha, the demon who threatened to dispossess the gods. Lakshmi, as the consort of Vishnu, was once reborn as one of the fourteen precious jewels from the churning of the milk ocean. In modern times, She has been worshipped on Her own as the goddess who brings affluence and prosperity. Sarasvati, as the consort of Brahma, is the Goddess of poetry, music, and higher learning. She is also a great linguist who invented the Sanskrit language.

Although these gods and goddesses appear separate and are even worshipped separately, they are creations of one God. This message of universal love and unified consciousness is essential for our enlightenment as human beings. We spend too much time and energy in pursuing separate paths and making each path look different; we ignore the fact that all spiritual paths lead to the same destination.

Spiritual endeavour is also an attempt at self-realization. Sacred words are essential at the start of the journey because we need to visualize the process of self-transformation. But once we are far ahead in our pursuits, we are gripped by an overbearing passion of divine love. It starts living in our thoughts and recollections. Every breath is sanctified by the presence of the Lord. Every action is guided by clear light. Our entire being is transformed by the intensity of our goal-driven emotions.

6

Going Beyond Simple Ritualism

Tirath naavaa jay tis bhaavaa vin bhaanay ke naa-ay karii.

Jaytii sirath upaa-ii vaykhaa vin karmaa ke milai la-ii.

Mat vich ratan javaahar maanik jay ik gur kii sikh sunii.

Guraa ik dayhei bujhaa-ii.

Sabhnaa jii-aa kaa ik daataa so mai visar na jaa-ii.

Holy bathing is fruitless if His pleasure is not obtained.

The divine creation that I behold is not without action attained.

With His guidance, the hidden mental treasure is regained.

Guru gave me one word of enlightenment:

there is only one God of all creation, let me not forget.

This meditation explains the importance of grace and true potentiality. The traditional religions of India prescribe taking a sacred journey to bathe in holy rivers. Although this is easy, particularly for people who have the money to go on such trips, there is no guarantee that these actions by themselves are sufficient to be rewarding in any manner. And if the Supreme is not pleased, they are wasteful efforts.

If we sincerely desire atonement, we have to make a greater effort than simply making ritualistic offerings. It calls for sustained periods of meditation. It entails remembrance of the Name. It means setting high moral standards for our life. Being and doing are inseparable. What is required is a perfect alignment between our personal and public behaviours. God sees through all falsehood. Keeping an outward appearance of piety is meaningless.

There is a reference in this meditation to human potential. Hidden inside all of us is a container holding the treasury of jewels (our potential). These jewels are much more precious than those we know and value. The hidden jewels symbolize our divinity and our ability to ask for and receive God's love. God has not given up on this creation. We have forgotten God in our attempt to gain worldly power, fame, and fortune. Even those who commit serious crimes have the potential to ask for forgiveness. It is never too late to get back on the right path. But this cannot happen until we become conscious of our true potential.

Because the hidden treasure is hard to reach when it is covered by weeds, our hidden treasure remains inaccessible if we allow the dust of our actions to settle on it. Of course, there is always time, and we could postpone this discovery to our last day. But prayer, in that case, will be self-serving. God sees and weighs our intentions on the scales of eternity before giving us another chance to redeem ourselves. We can cross the gulf between death and immortality if we ceaselessly work towards it.

7

The Cycle of Yugas

Jay jug chaaray aarjaa hor dasoonii ho-ay.
Navaa khanda vich jaanii-ai naal chalai sabh ko-ay.
Changa naa-o rakhaa-ay kai jas kiirat jag lay-ay.
Jay tis nadar na aavii ta vaat na puchhai kay.
Kiitaa andar kiit kar dosii dos dharay.
Naanak nirgun gun karay gunvanti-aa gun day.
Tayhaa ko-ay na sujh-ee je tis gun ko-ay karay.

Even if our lifespan covers four ages times ten.
Even if we gain nine continents, with everything on our side.
Even if our good name and deeds have won us worldly recognition.
Without His blessing and grace, all this adds up to nothing.
We will be the lowest of all beings.
O Nanak, the unmerited can gain true merit
and with His grace they can become truly virtuous!
But is there anyone who can bestow any virtue on the Lord?

We pray for a long life. But how long could our lifespan be? This meditation suggests a limit of four ages times ten. What is the significance of four ages? According to Hindu mythology, Brahma creates the universe, and it takes one full day of four and one-third million years to do the job. When the work of creation is done, Brahma sleeps for a period that lasts an equal amount of time. The universe is manifested and it runs its course in four ages or yugas—Krita/ Satya (the Golden Age, lasting nearly two million years), Treta (lasting nearly one million years, in which virtue has already started to disappear),

Dwapara (lasting less than one million years, in which virtue is only half present), and Kali (the present age of degeneration that started with Sri Krishna's death and will last less than one-half million years; it is marked by slavery, degradation, oppression, famines, and wars).

The Kali Yuga, or the age of Kali, will end with the coming of the Kalki, the tenth and last incarnation of Vishnu, who will destroy the wicked and prepare the ground for the renewal of creation. Then Shiva will come out of His cave to do Tandava (the greatest dance of all) that destroys the universe.

Since each of these ages consists of thousands of years, living for this length of time is beyond our imagination. Even if it is possible to have our life spread over such vast periods, it will not serve any useful purpose. What could be the purpose of such a life if it is devoid of divine love? What is important is not the length of time we live, but what we do with our lives. A short life filled with divine love is worth more than a long life lived in pursuit of other attractions. The meditation draws our attention to the fallacy of fame and wealth. It is not wrong to be rich or famous. Only those who are divinely blessed have material abundance in life. Riches and fame should not distract us from living a meditative life. Once we start accepting material things as the sole end of our life, however, spiritual degeneration becomes inevitable. A life free from God's presence is worthless; it would be a diversion from our primary goal. It is the kind of life that is led by creatures at the lower end of the evolutionary scale.

The selections we make are essential because the choice of being nearer to God is open to all of us. Our past actions do not stand in the way of renewing ourselves. God gives us the freedom to start all over again at every juncture of our life. We can hear the call if we sharpen our perception of differentiating the real from the unreal.

8

Listening to the Word

Suni-ai sidh piir sur naath.
Suni-ai dharat dhaval aakaas.
Suni-ai diip lo-a paataal.
Suni-ai pohi na sakai kaal.
Naanak bhagtaa sadaa vigaas.
Suni-ai dookh paap kaa naas.

Listening, we become spiritually realized beings and yogis.
Listening, we know this earth, a mythical bull, and the skies.
Listening, we discover hidden worlds and regions.
Listening, we conquer death's legions.
O Nanak, those who believe are always in a blissful state!
Listening to the Word, our sorrows and sins negate.

When we listen to a prayer, we remember God and our senses are filled with spiritual energy. Remembrance is not only a memory that comes alive; it is a feast for our body, mind, and soul. We witness the miracle of unfolding mysteries, including mythological revelations such as the earth being balanced on the horns of a bull. We overcome the fear of death. We attain bliss experienced by a true yogi. Just this one act of hearing the Name makes our sins disappear. The Word (*shabad* or *gurbani*) should be the starting point of our meditation. It is no ordinary name; it conveys the qualities of omnipresence and omniscience. Listening to the Name is also remembrance.

Remembrance of God does not necessarily involve painful meditation in lonely places. There is a simple meditation that is equally effective: listening to or reciting the Word. Any place or any time is right for it. Such is the power and beauty of God's name that even lending our ears to it could make a difference. We can gain wisdom, saintliness, and contentment. If listening to the Word is so profitable, we can imagine what rewards would come our way if we dedicate our lives to the pursuit of this goal.

Listening to the Word has other benefits too. Our body is so small compared with the vastness that surrounds us. This should not worry us because we do not stand apart from the earth and the sky. What is within us—our subatomic structure—is also what is outside. But the realization of this unity could come only through the power of the Word. When we listen to the Word, it is also heard by other beings, stones, particles, and matter, elements that are in perpetual motion in the cosmic vastness. It is the Word that binds us to the rest of the universe. We are no longer small, isolated, insignificant beings. We become partners in the magic of creation.

Listening to the Word puts us in touch with what is below the surface of this earth: infernal regions that are symbolic of the underworld, or the four lower planes of nature ruled by Greek gods such as Pluto. This is the region that is commonly associated with hell, Hades, or Sheol (mentioned in the Hebrew Bible). It is not only a place for tormenting lower-level beings, but also for purifying them in the eternal fires that burn there all the time. We need not have any fear of these regions and hellfire if we listen to the Name, as we shall be purified without any exposure to these fires.

Gurbani frees us from fear of all kinds. We are no longer afraid of the power of tyrants, ugly beasts, or ghosts. *Gurbani* gives us our true freedom. A life without fear is a life filled with the love of God. Listening to *gurbani* makes God dwell within us. Sorrow and pain cannot touch us ever again.

9

Inner Transformation by Listening to the Word

Suni-ai iisar barmaa ind.
Suni-ai mukh saalaahan mand.
Suni-ai jog jugat tan bhayd.
Suni-ai saasat simrit vayd.
Naanak bhagtaa sadaa vigaas.
Suni-ai duukh paap kaa naas.

Listening, Shiva, Brahma, and Indra were transformed.
Listening, even lower beings are divinely ordained.
Listening, we understand yogic mysteries.
Listening, we acquire scriptural secrets.
O Nanak, those who believe are always in a blissful state!
Listening, our sorrows and sins negate.

Personal transformation can occur through meditation. We can develop within ourselves the power and the spiritual reach of gods and goddesses. In a blissful state, pain and suffering do not affect us. When we think of God, we see the glorious manifestation of sublime beauty in everything. Ordinary human beings can attain total transformation if they recite the Name. Shiva, Brahma, and Indra are symbols of divine power. Shiva enjoys a unique place in Hindu mythology, given His many roles as a fearsome destroyer, lover, and ascetic, but He is very often a quarrelsome deity. Brahma is the creator of the universe, first among all the gods, God of wisdom, and the wellspring of the Vedas. Indra is God of storms and thunderbolts that

He uses to destroy the demons. He also brings rain, which is essential for human survival and prosperity.

One can imagine the combined sweep of divine power that these deities possess. We might wonder about the insignificance of an ordinary human being when compared with these powerful deities. Guru Nanak uses names of these gods as metaphors for the extraordinary power that can be attained if we embrace the purity, beauty, and sublimity of the Name.

It is generally believed that God's compassion is reserved for the virtuous and the truthful. Those who lead sinful lives, commit murders, and torment other human beings; those who live for themselves and have hearts devoid of any feelings for the suffering of others are not worthy of divine compassion. This meditation presents another viewpoint. All human beings are worthy of divine mercy at any point of time in their lives, provided they change themselves, give up the life of greed and lust, and genuinely pray for atonement.

An active listener is one who absorbs the purity of the Word and allows oneself to be transformed into a new person. A passive listener, on the other hand, does not make any effort and is possibly still numbed by worldly desires. For an active listener, hearing the Word in itself brings out the hidden magic. We are no longer limited physically or hopelessly tyrannized by our karma. The Word gives back to us our freedom to attain our higher potential, and we are gradually raised to a level where we become worthy of divine praise reserved for gods like Shiva, Brahma, and Indra.

The Word not only grants us spiritual merit but also unfolds the secrets of our inner being. One reason that we act indifferently towards our soul and its needs is because we are unaware of our spiritual possibilities. We know ourselves as desirous beings and for our shortcomings like anger, violence, greed, and self-centredness. We ignore the fact that we are also pure souls, informed and guided by God at every stage in our life. To be unaware of this divine presence is a sin of ignorance.

The source of ultimate wisdom lies in our scriptures, our sacred traditions, and religious texts. We must gain this wisdom and benefit fully from it. This life is an opportunity for attaining enlightenment. But we need help to muddle through the path of our actions. If we are not ready to take the first step, the rest of the way is closed for us. It is only through listening to our inner voice that we can gain momentum to go any further on this path.

10

The Real Magic of Listening to the Word

Suni-ai sat santokh gi-aan.
Suni-ai athsath kaa isnaan.
Suni-ai parh parh paavahi maan.
Suni-ai laagai sahj dhi-aan.
Naanak bhagtaa sadaa vigaas.
Suni-ai duukh paap kaa naas.

Listening, we gain truth, contentment, and discernment.
Listening, we bathe at sixty-eight places of sacrament.
Listening, we gain veneration and admiration.
Listening, we attain poised meditation.
O Nanak, those who believe are always in a blissful state!
Listening, our sorrows and sins negate.

The expression of love for God is a tremendous transformational act. We can see the difference it makes in our life. It is like confessing—when we live for ourselves, happiness eludes us; when we live for others, we are stranded alone and lied to and cheated by friends and relatives. Now, when we live for the love of the Lord, we are embraced by truth and goodness. Nothing passes by this great source of light without being transformed.

Human existence can be viewed along a spectrum of darkness and light. At the lower levels, we are devoid of truth, contentment, and discernment or right perception. Some people who have no reservations about lying, lie or cheat to achieve their objectives, notwithstanding the damage their lies or cheating would do to their victims. Because lies are difficult to disprove, these people can even portray themselves as 'victims', deserving of sympathy.

Liars have one thing in common, however. They live in perpetual spiritual darkness. They lead miserable lives, unaware of their misery, the real suffering of their souls. However, they are capable of dragging themselves out of this darkness by subjecting themselves to a new routine in their lives. When they move to the other side of the spectrum, they are informed by truth, contentment, and accurate perception.

It is common for people to perform ritualistic acts as a measure of self-purification. They seek forgiveness by subjecting themselves to enormous physical inconvenience, such as by journeying to faraway places. This meditation shows us the right way to find atonement, which does not involve any journey or ritual or financial expense. It requires us to listen to *gurbani* with devotion and single-mindedness. We do not have to leave our home to go anywhere because God is omnipresent. If we cannot find the object of our love in our place, we will not find it anywhere.

Divinity brings us wisdom. In every society, wise people are respected. Those who have attained wisdom are keenly followed because other people wish to share their knowledge and want to listen to what they have to say. Such admiration must be accepted with great humility. Because we are not perfect, praises often inflate our egos and we may make claims of saintliness while we are still mired in the world of desire. In the end, all honour belongs to God. Those who show this understanding will be remembered as pure devotees.

Another attribute of wisdom is achieving scholarly distinction. To undertake academic work requires several years of education followed by specialization in a scientific discipline. Irrespective of the subject of study, all scholarly pursuits are divinely inspired. People who change the world for better through their work act as divine agents. Without divine inspiration, no discovery can be made. Real scientists know the limits of tools used to test new hypotheses. They appreciate God's grand design for the universe and its beings, as reflected in Einstein's famous quip, 'God does not play dice.'

Listening to *gurbani* is essential for people who do manual work as well as those who create new scientific knowledge. Real achievement awaits only those who work with humility and pursue their work as a form of meditation. If we forget the Name, our labour could be instrumental in creating a gas chamber or weapons of mass destruction. In all of human history, tyrants were empowered to commit acts of brutality by people who used their craft in ways that were not consistent with any divine purpose. This happens even today in many places, which is why this message is of immediate relevance.

Meditation reminds us about the everlasting bliss that awaits those who can absorb the Name. They are saved from suffering and sin. In divine wardship, there is only one state of being: true and everlasting bliss.

11

Listening Both with the Heart and the Mind

Suni-ai saraa gunaa kay gaah.
Suni-ai saykh piir paatisaah.
Suni-ai andhay paavahi raahu.
Suni-ai haath hovai asgaahu.
Naanak bhagtaa sadaa vigaas.
Suni-ai duukh paap kaa naas.

Listening makes us attain an ocean of virtues.
Listening brightens our minds,
and makes us spiritual guides and mentors.
Listening makes the spiritually blind find a way.
By listening, fathomless deep truths come under our sway.
O Nanak, those who believe are always in a blissful state!
Listening, our sorrows and sins negate.

As one of the most beautiful creations of God, human beings are empowered to be virtuous. The sacred within us does not readily admit evil in any form. But for several practical reasons, we are quick to lose touch with our divinity. Once this happens, we accept in principle that accommodation with the evil is possible. The worldly attractions, coupled with the power of our ego-mind, are such that we allow the ocean of virtue to diminish. Our eyes cannot see the true self within us. The inner eye, to see virtue's ocean, has to be developed anew through a slow and arduous process of atonement. We have to regularly listen to the Name to unravel the mystery of our hidden self.

The listening process implied here is not passive. Some people believe that listening or hearing means lending our ears to something—the external stimuli pouring into our head. That is not what is suggested here. Listening, in this case, means listening as well as learning. It implies that sensory input is compelling us to search for meaning, thereby awakening our mental abilities to differentiate one sense from another. It also means that we use our heart as well as our mind, logic, and intuition. The mind alone, as the centre of our rational self, lacks the emotional energy to understand the spiritual and mystical undertones of the divine message. Therefore, we have to listen with our heart as well as our mind. We have to capture the meaning as well as the mystery of the message.

Listening to the Name gives us wisdom. It is not the wisdom of being worldly-wise but the wisdom of knowing the ultimate reality, the knowledge that will eventually bring us closer to enlightenment. The reference here is to the wisdom of great shaikhs and pirs in the mystical Sufi tradition. Sufis are known to practice zikr, meaning remembrance, which involves chanting the name of God as part of their prayer and meditation. Through this process, they experience the extinction of their ego (*fana*), which occurs when the mystic attains a perfect union with God. The difference between 'I' and 'Thou' disappears, and the self becomes part of the divine. As the Sufi poet Rumi said, 'This moment this love comes to rest in me, many beings in one being. In one wheat-grain a thousand sheaf stacks. Inside the needle's eye, a turning night of the stars.'[1]

When we recite the Name, the voice comes from within. In a way, we are listening to our voice. But this is no ordinary voice; it is the voice wrapped within a great mystery. The awareness of what is within and what is outside starts disappearing as we reach deeper meditative

---

1   Coleman Barks, *The Illuminated Rumi* (New York: Broadway Books, 1997), p. 99.

states. Slowly we learn to put ourselves out of the way and merge into the cosmic cycle that connects our ordinary self with the universal consciousness.

Listening to the Name enables us to overcome our blindness. Again, the meditation does not refer to a physical condition, although miracles do happen to cure physical ailments. This blindness is the blindness of the soul, our inability to see the spiritual nature of our being, and our potential to attain higher levels of consciousness. Only when we overcome our spiritual blindness are we able to see. This will happen when we start listening to the Name and start abiding by its discipline.

Listening to the Name, we shall come to know both the fathomable and unfathomable mysteries of our existence. The fathomable part of our self is more natural to know. It is like knowing our conscious mind. The unfathomable part is much more profound; to find it, we have to delve not only into our 'personal unconscious' but into the unknown mysteries of the 'collective unconscious', as explained by the Swiss psychologist Carl Jung. The unfathomable space is the seat or centre of our soul. To be in touch with it is to reach the core of our spiritual being—the highest ambition we can carry in our heart.

Listening to the Name confers special blessings. We can live in an eternally blissful state. Such is the power of the Name that suffering of all kinds and sinful actions disappear. Where there is the Name, there is no suffering, there is no sin. Our pain is caused by moving away from God and indulging ourselves in the world of desire, wealth, and fame, mainly driven by our ego-mind. In these pursuits, mental stress is bound to be our companion because we do not wish to fail. We stretch ourselves to the limits of our physical and mental capacities, and then one day the chord breaks. It breaks because there is nothing to support it. The glue of the Word can bind us to our inner reality so that even when we are pursuing our goals, we will not find ourselves distant from the eternal bliss.

12

A State of Bliss Beyond Words

Mannay kii gat kahii na jaa-ay.
Jay ko kahai pichhai pachhutaa-ay.
Kaagad kalam na likhanhaar.
Mannay kaa bahi karan viichaar.
Aisaa naam niranjan ho-ay.
Jay ko man jaanai man ko-ay.

A believer's bliss is hard to recount.
Anyone who tries to explain this, regrets.
There is no paper, pen, or penmanship to describe
the believer's bliss and worship.
Such is the power of His immaculate denomination,
that we know it only through total submission.

The state of self-realization (oneness with the Supreme Self) is hard to describe because it is an experience that transcends all human sensory experiences. Any such attempt will be futile because what we have not yet experienced cannot be captured in words. Words can easily miscommunicate and misinform, not so much by conscious design as by the sheer inadequacy of the language itself. Experience is always more intense than its expression.

What is written on paper is an outward expression of an inner state. No pen has the power to write down words that accurately reflect the emotional state of a follower. The scholarship needed to capture the essence of such experience cannot be cultivated. It has to be divinely gifted. The real test is the unshakable faith in the divine reality and its manifestation. There is an actual state of sublime bliss that comes only after continuous and deep meditation of the Name. Not through flights of fancy or magical tricks but only through one's reflection is this spiritual energy released.

As the Name is purity itself, human actions need to be exemplary to earn divine grace. This outcome is reached through total submission of one's intent to attain the soul's higher aspirations.

13

The Essence of True Wisdom

Mannai surat hovai man budh.
Mannai sagal bhavan kii sudh.
Mannai muhi chotaa naa khaa-ay.
Mannai jam ke saath na jaa-ay.
Aisaa naam niranjan ho-ay.
Jay ko man jaanai man ko-ay.

A believer gains wisdom, consciousness, and awareness.
A believer gains inner and outer mindfulness.
A believer does not go stumbling and hobbling.
A believer is not terrorized by death's calling.
Such is the power of His immaculate denomination,
that we know it only through total submission.

Our faith in the divine order gives us numerous gifts: wisdom, consciousness, understanding, and mindfulness. Our mind is opened to extraordinary experiences. We overcome the fear of death, and we become conscious of the real potential of our soul. There is a multitude of gifts for us to possess and cherish. This meditation describes some of them.

First and foremost, there is the gift of wisdom, the expression of our higher mind. Wisdom here has a different meaning than what is commonly understood. A wise person is said to be one who knows the ways of the world, or who can grasp technical or professional knowledge. That kind of wisdom is essential and is also a divine gift, but there is a pearl of higher wisdom based on truth, love, and right living. It is the wisdom that makes us aware of the ultimate cause and effect. Where do we come from and where do we go? What are the various cycles of births and deaths that we have already completed? What forms of life have we already inhabited? What is the broad direction of our evolution? How could we hasten our movement towards our final destination? How are we to lead our life so that we become worthy of divine love?

The answers to these questions are not simple, but we have the option to follow the dictates of the Name and to place our trust in the divine will. We have to become instruments to spread love and compassion, remembering our Creator with every breath we take and keeping our body clean and healthy so that the abode of the soul is clean and healthy. This is the essence of divine wisdom, a wisdom that is a precondition of enlightenment.

Consciousness or awareness is another divine gift. Self-knowledge is essential to our spiritual life. This is the only quality that separates the living from the dead. But the real gift here is the higher consciousness, a state of mind that enables us to distinguish the real from the unreal, truth from the falsehood, permanent from the transient, spirit from the matter, and here and now from the eternal. Once we attain this level of consciousness, death ceases to be any threat to our being. We get to know the true identity of our soul-self that has always lived and will never cease to be.

A truly realized person has the consciousness to fathom the inner reaches of the self. Our inner awareness is a reflection of what is outside, the physical reality that can be seen with our eyes and touched by our hands. But once we attain a higher level of consciousness, the difference between inside and outside tends to disappear. We can see ourselves as the projection of a larger whole, active participants in the miracle of this divine creation. Our breath is the subtle connection between these two realities. The air that we breathe brings the promise of life. The air that we exhale is an act of meditation, an invisible salute to the divine mystery, a mixing of particles that were once part of ourselves with the universal flow of energy. This realization—that the inner and outer realities exist as interdependent conditions, each enriching the other—is at the very heart of mindful living.

The test of our true belief is the stability of our mind and action. An unstable mind is a dangerous companion, meaninglessly meandering from one object to the other. Volatile responses are always half-hearted. We do things that do not appeal to us. We follow paths unaware of their final destinations. But once we come to accept the reality of our being and the total sweep of the divine power, once we subdue our ego and submit ourselves to the dictates of God, our mind becomes stable and peaceful and our actions become a model for others to follow.

A true believer has no fear of death or dying. Our physical end is a new beginning—our chance to attain immortality, an opportunity to live in the presence of the Lord. Our 'death' in this life can bring us freedom from the pains of subsequent births and deaths. This is an opportunity, but can we make this transition? Much depends on what we do in this life. If we have allowed *gurbani* to become a part of our being, if we have put absolute trust in the will of God, if we have done things right and have spoken well, our chances of entry into the higher realm are brightened. If our life is spent in the pursuit of worldly pleasures, we will be unable to avoid the cycle of birth and death with the pain and suffering that accompanies.

14

One True Path

Mannai maarag thaak na paa-ay.
Mannai pat si-o pargat jaa-ay.
Mannai mag na chalai panth.
Mannai dharam saytee san-bandh.
Aisaa naam niranjan ho-ay.
Jay ko man jaanai man ko-ay.

A believer's path is unfettered and self-directing.
A believer departs this world with honour and lauding.
A believer does not stray into ritualistic sects.
A believer follows righteous associates.
Such is the power of His immaculate denomination,
that we know it only through total submission.

A believer's spiritual path is straightforward; there are no obstacles, no barriers. There is only one goal. Sideshows hold no attractions. There are no sights and sounds that distract attention. Such single-mindedness and passionate pursuit of a single goal is the result of an inner urge, an internal flow of energy that keeps the believer moving in the same direction at all times. Every milestone is a step closer to God. There may be temporary setbacks, but a true believer's faith is never lost. And hope cannot be lost if divine acclaim is earned every step of the way. Meandering tracks, although deceptively attractive to look at, hold no fascination for this traveller. The sense of duty and the courage of one's convictions are so strong that total submission to the dictates of divine reality is not forgotten.

How is one to find the correct path and follow it? By making virtue our ally. When we become virtuous, the path shows itself. There is no need to search for it because virtue is an anchor that does not allow us to go astray. By obeying God, one proceeds in ecstasy on His path. And how does one obey God? By leading a virtuous life, which means having right thoughts and actions, a sense of humility, a willingness to share one's wealth and skills with others, and a heart filled with the love of God.

The Gate to Enlightenment

Mannai paavahi mokh du-aar.
Mannai parvaarai saadhaar.
Mannai tarai taaray gur sikh.
Mannai Naanak bhavahi na bhikh.
Aisaa naam niranjan ho-ay.
Jay ko man jaanai man ko-ay.

A believer gains entry through the gate to enlightenment and
    immortality.
A believer helps and improves others.
A believer liberates self and others seeking spiritual fulfilment.
A believer, says Nanak, does not have to wander for divine grace!
Such is the power of His immaculate denomination,
that we know it only through total submission.

A true believer has no problem in attaining a soul life, a state that assures the most considerable freedom of all—the freedom from being and non-being. Such is the blessed state of the mind of the person who achieves enlightenment that it even impacts the lives of friends and relatives, and others. They, too, can become divinely blessed through this act of association with a true believer.

This meditation assures us that the rewards for keeping one's faith are many and truly enriching. Not only are the doors to eternal happiness and bliss opened, but there is no shortage of material possessions either. These possessions may not hold much attraction for a person in search of the divine, but they can make a difference in determining the comfort level in which spiritual interests are pursued. Only a true believer can reap this harvest.

There are several related arguments in this meditation. First, if we have true faith, we shall find the path to the liberation of our soul. Second, once we see these openings, we can not only cross into a new dimension of time and space but can help our loved ones to do so too. Third, true faith liberates not only the disciple but also the preceptor, who is our guru or mentor. When the disciple takes one step closer to God, the preceptor also advances as a true liberator of souls. Fourth and the last, when we firmly maintain our faith, we no longer wander in search of divine grace. It is bestowed on us every step of the way.

16

Mysteries of the Created Universe

Panch parvaan panch pardhaan.
Panchay paavahi dargahi maan.
Panchay sohahi dar raajaan.
Panchaa kaa gur ayk dhi-aan.
Jay ko kahai karai viichaar.
Kartay kai karnai naahii sumaar.
Dhoul dharam da-i-aa kaa puut.
Santokh thaap rakhi-aa jin suut.
Jay ko bujhai hovai sachiaar.
Dhavlai upar kaytaa bhaar.
Dhartee hor parai hor hor.
Tis tay bhaar talai kavan jor.
Jii-a jaat rangaa kay naav.
Sabhnaa likhi-aa vurhii kalaam.
Ayhu laykhaa likh jaanai ko-ay.
Laykhaa likhi-aa kaytaa ho-ay.
Kaytaa taan su-aalihu ruup.
Kaytee daat jaanai koun kuut.
Keetaa pasaa-o ayko kavaa-o.
Tis tay ho-ay lakh daree-aa-o.
Kudrat kavan kahaa veechaar.
Vaari-aa na jaavaa ayk vaar.
Jo tudh bhaavai saa-ee bhalee kaar.
Too sadaa salaamat Nirankaar.

They are blessed whom He selects.

They are honoured in His court.

They brighten the heavenly court with their spiritual fervour.

They find their minds centred in the meditation of His manor.

They try to describe Him after a good deal of reflection.

But His doings are beyond human enumeration.

Dharma's bull is born of compassion, and it holds the earth in
    equalization.

This discovery enlightens and makes us truthful.

How much load is carried by the mythical bull?

But there are planets and galaxies afar.

Who has carried their loads so far?

There are different species and colours they enshrine,

written by the ever-flowing pen of the Supreme Lord.

Does anyone know how complete the full account might be?

If an account is written, how extensive might that be?

How powerful is the measure of His manifestation?

Who can estimate the greatness of His benediction?

He created the universe with a single injunction,

and there emerged many a flowing river and inundation.

What power do I have to describe Lord's creation?

My powerlessness precludes even a simple act of sacrifice!

Whatever pleases Him is the noble deed.

Forever eternal and formless!

Truly honoured are those who are divinely selected. They understand the secrets of creation—of natural and physical phenomena like birds, flowering trees, and rivers. Ordinary human beings have no power to describe creation in this manner. Our strength stems only from the Creator. If it does not come as a divine gift, it does not come at all.

This meditation is exceptionally beautiful. It covers an immense range of themes. It talks about our moral and intellectual development, spiritual awakening, environmental ethics, and our relationship with the Creator and the creation.

Those who are chosen by God are morally and intellectually superior. They have their minds fixed on God. They do not think about anything else. Nothing else matters to them.

The basis of the divine law is love and compassion, which we need to understand in dynamic terms. Love and compassion are the foundations of divine actions, but these are not static constructs. They are more like flows of positive energy, fountains, or springs from which mercy, affection, and acceptance continue uninterrupted for the benefit of all creation. All beings, therefore, are eligible for a second or a third chance. It is never too late for us to seek atonement. And whenever we come forward, our call is answered.

Once we understand and accept these simple truths, our mind is opened to the mysteries of creation mythology. Whether our planet stands on the horns of a mythical bull, or is part of a complex array of solar systems and galaxies, we are sure to discover the truth. Who controls this vast universe? Whose command extends over these intergalactic distances that are difficult to measure and nearly impossible to explain? Did it all start with a 'big bang', the singular explosion of energy at the beginning of the creation of this universe? Will it all end in a 'big crunch', a massive contraction of all energy when this universe comes to an end? Who created black holes from which nothing, not even light, can escape? Can we ever discover these secrets?

The meditation shows us a path of discovery. This discovery is not separate from the revelation of God, because, in reality, the Creator and the creation are one. There are no secrets that are hidden from the sight of a true believer. It is the power of our faith that opens all these doors to mystical realms that are hidden from our eyes.

This meditation celebrates biodiversity. There are so many creatures on this planet that their number is beyond any intelligent guess. Even the best research scientists have no answer to the question of how much exists, how much has already become extinct, and how much is in the process of evolving into other forms. Is this all happening by chance, as the unfolding of a Darwinian horror story? The question is also an answer to resolving the mystery of creation. Nothing happens by chance. Science can explain some parts, but it has to leave some others to speculation.

The current debate about the preservation of biodiversity misses one essential point. Biodiversity needs to be preserved not only for its medicinal, recreational, educational, and scientific values (all these goals are vital by themselves), but also because we have no right to destroy this divine creation. It is only God who has the absolute power to kill something or to keep it alive. Human interference in these matters is a violation of the divine law.

The unconditional acceptance of the divine will is the first step towards our self-awareness and spiritual awakening. Nature can be a great teacher and healer in our quest. Creation is not separate from the Creator, in the same way as any work of art is inseparable from the artist. But this is a limiting analogy. It is not just a work of art, confined to a small space in an art gallery. We are talking about an act of creation whose boundaries over space and time are unfathomable. This complexity is irreducible to any simple hypothesis. We can use science or logic to unfold this, but there is no better tool than the practice of meditation. Once we experience self-awakening and allow the divine flow of energy to radiate to the darkest reaches of our soul, the mysteries of creation will slowly unfold.

17

Different Ways to Connect with the Lord

Asankh jap asankh bhaa-o.
Asankh puujaa asankh tap taa-o.
Asankh garanth mukh vayd paath.
Asankh jog man rahahi udaas.
Asankh bhagat gun gi-aan viichaar.
Asankh satii asankh daataar.
Asankh suur muh bhakh saar.
Asankh mon liv laa-ay taar.
Kudrat kavan kahaa viichaar.
Vaari-aa na jaavaa ek vaar.
Jo tudh bhaavai saa-ii bhalii kaar.
Too sadaa salaamat Nirankaar.

Countless are meditations and countless are ways of atonement.
Countless are scriptures and countless those who are spiritual
    seekers.
Countless are yogis who are indifferent to worldly encounters.
Countless are devotees who ponder on things veritable.
Countless are kind and those who are charitable.
Countless are warriors who face the wrath
    of their opposition.
Countless are worshipers who believe in silent contemplation.
What power do I have to describe Lord's creation?
My powerlessness precludes even a simple act of sacrifice!
Whatever pleases Him is the noble deed.
Always eternal and formless.

There are different ways of worship. Differences between individuals are reflected in the ways they connect with God. There are those of us who are satisfied with merely saying our prayers. But some are not content with this. They think that their prayer is incomplete without inflicting physical suffering on themselves. This suffering can take several forms: fasting, sitting in a particular body posture for extended periods, inflicting pain through various other means, including sleeping on hard floors. There are those who read the holy scriptures and meditate to satisfy their spiritual quest. And there are others who needlessly inflict pain on themselves, thinking that God would be pleased to see them suffer. These are all misperceptions. How could the source of greatest love and compassion ever wish to inflict pain on us?

There is no need to go through rituals involving pain and discomfort. Nothing matters except the purity of one's prayer. When the Name comes to our lips from the inner reaches of our soul, that by itself becomes the best form of worship.

A distinction is made here between two forms of worship—one based on knowledge and the other on love. We can use our intellect to reflect on the nature of God. We can ask questions and answer them with the power of our mind. This is what philosophers are trained to do. They can handle abstractions, using their mental models to conceptualize what is known and what is unknown. This is a form of worship, but perhaps it is not suited to everyone's needs.

The other mode of worship is relatively simple: it is based on love. In this mode, there is no need to ask questions. There are no questions. When one's heart is filled with love and compassion, there is nothing more to be known. There is no place for any doubt; there is no room for any scepticism. The path of love is the most direct and the most accessible way to enlightenment. God is love as well as the truth. When we love God without any qualifiers, we get pure and unalloyed love that is true and eternal.

The worship of God is the fundamental right of all beings. It has nothing to do with the state of evolution of one's body or mind. Birds sing and animals howl as their way of celebrating the glory of this creation. Human beings are indeed more complicated. They express their devotion in different ways. Sometimes, the rich and powerful feel that they have a greater right to display their faith than those who are poor. These are misconceptions. In our relationship with God, all of us stand on the same footing. Our stature might differ according to our spiritual evolution, but material things have no significance. It is true that the rich can travel more easily to holy lands than the poor, but that begs the question: is there a place on earth which is not sacred? When we close our eyes and feel the presence of God, we sanctify the ground on which we stand. This experience does not cost any money; it needs only our readiness to embrace our Creator. When we are ready, God shows us the way.

18

Divine Love is Available for All Seekers

Asankh muurakh andh ghor.
Asankh chor haraamkhor.
Asankh amar kar jaahi jor.
Asankh galvadh hati-aa kamaahi.
Asankh paapii paap kar jaahi.
Asankh kuurhi-aar kuurhay firaahi.
Asankh malaychh mal bhakh khaahi.
Asankh nindak sir karahi bhaar.
Naanak niich kahai viichaar.
Vaari-aa na jaavaa ek vaar.
Jo tudh bhaavai saa-ee bhalee kaar.
Too sadaa salaamat Nirankaar.

Countless are fools who are appallingly ignorant of divine knowledge.
Countless are thieves who are disgustingly repugnant.
Countless are tyrants who command others with force before they
      depart this world.
Countless are those who cut throats and commit murders.
Countless are sinners who lead sinful lives.
Countless are liars who wander in their own falsehoods.
Countless are wretches who have impure minds and live in filthy bins.
Countless are slanderers who will carry the burden of their sins.
Nanak humbly expresses this thought:
My powerlessness precludes even a simple act of sacrifice!
Whatever pleases the Lord is a noble deed.
Always eternal and formless.

Some people lead lowly forms of life. They are unaware that this life has been gifted to them after a long evolutionary struggle. This is the time when they can get closer to God, but because they are spiritually deficient, they do not know the opportunities they are missing. We do not need a degree in divinity for God realization. We need wisdom that is wisdom of the heart—knowing that the love of God is available to us when we want it.

Some people steal and rob. They take away what does not belong to them from their innocent victims. They think that they can get away with cheating. They are ignorant because they do not see the reach of the divine law. No offensive action goes unpunished, in the same way that no good work goes unrewarded. There may be a delay in divine justice, but there is no avoiding it.

Some autocratic leaders or tyrants oppress their people and deny them fundamental human rights. Political oppression does not last forever, however. It can cast a long shadow and dishearten many, but not those who have faith in God's mercy and a belief in the final victory of good over evil. No tyrant lives forever. There is a moment of truth for every tyrant who thought that he could trample the world under his feet. Flames of love and hope that burn in the heart of a true believer can explode into the light of many suns when the merciful hand of God ends the reign of tyranny. Tyrants finally get a taste of their own medicine. They can lose their dignity and life at the hands of those whom they once oppressed.

When one leads a sinful life, or engages in lies, or talks ill of people who are God-fearing, such actions take us away from God. Once we go in the wrong direction on the path of ignorance, there is no hope for our redemption. We have to head in the right direction to find our own sacred space. The map we need for this purpose is the map of a loving heart. Then we shall never be lost because our path will always shine.

19

A Glimpse of the Divine Kingdom

Asankh naav asankh thaav.
Agamm agamm asankh lo-a.
Asankh kehahi sir bhaar ho-ay.
Akhrii naam akhrii saalaah.
Akhrii gi-aan giit gun gaah.
Akhrii likhan bolan baan.
Akhraa sir sanjog vakhaan.
Jin ayhi likhay tis sir naahi.
Jiv furmaa-ay tiv tiv paahi.
Jaytaa kiitaa taytaa naa-o.
Vin naavai naahee ko thaa-o.
Kudrat kavan kahaa viichaar.
Vaari-aa na jaavaa ek vaar.
Jo tudh bhaavai saa-ii bhalii kaar.
Too sadaa salaamat Nirankaar.

Countless are His names and countless are His abodes.
Beyond reach are His countless worlds and celestial modes.
To call these simply countless is a limiting description.
Through the Word, we chant His name and show our devotion.
Through the Word, we get knowledge and learn to sing His praises.
Through the Word is recorded our destiny and its mazes.
Yet these written words are not binding on Him.
What He decrees, we receive as His gift.
All creation is His manifestation and without Him there is no habitation.
What power do I have to describe the Lord's creation?

My powerlessness precludes even a simple act of sacrifice!
Whatever pleases the Lord is a noble deed.
Always eternal and formless!

This meditation provides a glimpse of the eternal kingdom. It is only a glimpse because the true glory of God is beyond words; it is revealed only to those who have earned the right to experience this grand vision.

Unlike human beings, who might have one or two names and dwellings, God has millions of names and abodes. Being in one place does not mean that He cannot be in other places. No place in this whole universe is free of divine presence.

God may be seen in various forms. These manifestations are without any limit. The blossoming of a flower, the flight of an eagle, the beauty of a lake, the roar of oceanic waves, and the notes of music floating in the air on a dark night—these are some of the manifestations of God's presence. Once we open our heart to the mysteries of this divine creation, we can gain access to God's limitless manifestations. Because we are constrained in terms of our reach and modes of expression, we pour out our love for Him through prayer and meditation. We have to depend on these modalities because we know of no other way of expressing ourselves. But once we are fully engrossed in our prayer, words are no longer words. Everything turns into a soul-transforming experience.

20

Body and Soul

Bharii-ai hath pair tan dayh.
Paanee dhotai utras khayh.
Muut paliitii kaparh ho-ay.
Day saaboon la-ii-ai oh dho-ay.
Bharii-ai mat paapaa kai sang.
Oh dhopai naavai kai rang.
Punnii paapii aakhan naahi.
Kar kar karnaa likh lai jaahu.
Aapay biij aapay hii khaahu.
Naanak hukmii aavhu jaahu.

When hands, feet, and body are covered with slime,
water washes, cleans, and purifies before time.
When clothes are soiled and emit foul smell,
a cake of soap clears the filth and makes them clean again.
When our mind is overlaid with sin and shame,
it will be cleansed only by the love of His name.
Saints and sinners are not made by being so-called.
Good and bad actions are known, and our future is destined.
As we sow, so shall we reap.
With divine will, O Nanak, this journey of life and death we repeat!

Our soul is a vehicle for the realization of God. But our body is spatially constrained; our hands reach out only a few feet. However, there is a part of us that is unbounded. We call it 'mind'—the centre of our consciousness. And, at the deepest level, there is the centre of our cosmic consciousness that we call our 'soul'. We know relatively little about our mind and even less about our soul. Scientists are exploring the extended power of the mind. Several studies about the power of prayer have shown that through what is called 'intercessory prayer', we can heal people who are miles away from us. This could not be possible unless our mind is part of an energy field that exerts influence over long distances. Our mind is not confined to our skull, like our brain; it is an extended substance whose real power we have yet to realize.

Whatever is known about the soul is the subject of considerable controversy. Does the soul exist? If so, where is it located? A straightforward way to describe the soul is to call it the 'essence' of our being that remains after our body is reduced to dust. It is the essence that continues to move on its journey of 'soul-making'. Our soul, not our body, meets with God, if and when we make this transition. God knows our essence; our earthly body that we leave behind has little significance. That is why this meditation highlights the importance of our soul and how we should nourish it in this life.

When our body is unclean, we can easily wash it with soap and fragrant liquids. When our clothes get dirty, they can be easily laundered. But when our soul is steeped in sin, when we have reached a level of sinfulness that has even soiled our soul, it cannot be washed by any earthly substance. No soap can clean it. The only thing that can help us in this endeavour is meditation. We can always ask for forgiveness for our actions, but to gain this realization, we need a period of reflection and recitation of the Name.

Along with this strict regimen of prayer and meditation, we have to watch our actions. What are we doing? Are we causing pain or suffering to others, or are we bringing happiness and joy?

According to the law of karma, every action has a reaction. The seeds of our actions will gradually fertilize; whether they are for our good or bad will depend on the nature of our efforts. Our good deeds enrich and nourish our soul; our harmful actions impoverish our soul. We can degrade ourselves to a level where we can brutalize or kill children without any sense of remorse, as is seen in many parts of the world today. On the other hand, a life of love and self-sacrifice, of devotion and compassion is uplifting. It raises our physical and moral stature. And more than anything else, it enhances the reach of our soul. Beyond the dazzling glare of the tunnel of light is the permanent abode of our soul. Are we foolishly going to miss this chance of reaching our goal?

21

Only the Creator Knows the Secret of Creation

Tirath tap da-i-aa dat daan.
Jay ko paavai til kaa maan.
Suni-aa mani-aa man kiitaa bhaa-o.
Antargat tirath mal naa-o.
Sabh gun tayray mai naahii ko-ay.
Vin gun kiitay bhagat na ho-ay.
Su-asat aath banee barmaa-o.
Sat suhaan sadaa man chaa-o.
Kavan so vaylaa vakhat kavan kavan thit kavan vaar.
Kavan se rutee maahu kavan jit ho-aa aakaar.
Vayl na paa-ii-aa pandtii je hovai laykh puraan.
Vakhat na paa-i-o kaadii-aa je likhan laykh kuraan.
Thit vaar naa jogii jaanai rut maahu naa ko-ii.
Jaa kartaa sirthii ka-o saajay aapay jaanai so-ii.
Kiv kar aakhaa kiv saalaahii ki-o varnii kiv jaanaa.
Naanak aakhan sabh ko aakhai ik duu ik si-aanaa.
Vadaa saahib vadee naa-ii kiitaa jaa kaa hovai.
Naanak jay ko aapou jaanai agai ga-i-aa na sohai.

Pilgrimage, atonement, compassion, and creed will fetch us merit,
if any, tiny as a seed of grain.
By hearing and by keeping in mind the Name, we get inner pilgrimage.
All virtue resides in Him, and none in me that others can see.
Without virtuous actions, none is a true devotee.
My salutation to Him, O creator of maya, and the sacred word
and Brahma the Creator!

Truth and beauty ever reside in His blissful heart and word.

What was the time, what hour, what date, and day of the week?

What was the season, what month did the Creator seek?

Pandit knows not the time, as it is not mentioned in the Purana.

Kazi knows not the time after reading the Koran.

Yogi knows not the day, season, or month of this calendar.

Only the Creator knows the intricacies of this cosmic grammar.

How should I address, describe this I know not?

Nanak, we offer discourses, call ourselves wise, but know not.

There is only one true Lord, who makes things happen.

Nanak, the pretentious will not have much glory to uncover!

There is sublime beauty and profound meaning to be found in this meditation. It gives us the secret of self-realization. It is not through any rituals that we realize God; it is not by making trips to holy lands; it is not through any number of outward actions that we get closer to God. All these actions, though good in practice, bring very minimal rewards. Total inner transformation is required. We have to love and adore the Lord with all our sincerity and goodness. We have to place everything at God's command, holding back nothing. Only then can we begin our spiritual journey—a journey of countless cosmic miles that starts with a simple resolve.

In the second part of this meditation, Guru Nanak comes back to God's grandeur and the mystery of creation. We enjoy talking about special moments in our lives: the time of our graduation, the day of our marriage, the time when we became a parent. These events are unique, but what about the event of creation itself? Can we compare what happens in the life of the universe with what happens in our lives? There is no comparison. However, it is humbling to remember how small our most joyous moments are compared to the most significant event of all—the creation of this universe itself.

Many people lay claim to this knowledge. They think that they know the secret. They are wrong. No one person knows it all. Nor is it written in any book. The mystery of creation resides solely in the mind of the Creator. No one else has any clue, but there are many good guesses. If we wish to share this secret, we have to aim at reaching a collective 'spiritual' consciousness to witness the amazing powers of this Creator.

22

Universe without Any Boundaries

Paataalaa paataal lakh aagaasaa aagaas.
Orhak orhak bhaal thakay vayd kahan ik vaat.
Sehas athaarah kahan kataybaa asuloo ik dhaat.
Laykhaa ho-ay ta likee-ai laykhai ho-ay vinaas.
Naanak vadaa aakhee-ai aapay jaanai aap.

Millions are the lower regions and countless spaces of unbounded
   vastness.
Wise ones have searched in vain, and the Vedas, too, declare
   helplessness.
Semitic texts count eighteen thousand, though there is only one
   essence.
His infinity none can measure; this search is of little consequence.
Only He, says Nanak, knows the Truth!

There are no visible limits to this universe. There are no boundaries of any kind. As we go further into outer space, we discover more and more. No end seems to exist. But the Creator, who created this universe, knows the answer—how it began and how it will end. All other answers are guesses. The work of the Creator can't be subjected to any human measurement. Our capacity to assess this phenomenon is inadequate.

God has many abodes. A literal translation of the opening line of this meditation would mean a hundred thousand worlds below and many heavens above! It is a limiting interpretation. As revealed by modern astrological sciences, the number of solar systems, galaxies, and stars is nearly limitless, beyond human calculation. It is precisely the point that this meditation wishes to convey. The count is futile because we can spend several lifetimes doing this calculation, and yet our count will not be complete. The 'wise' among us (should we call them 'scientists'?) can make claims, but their knowledge is incomplete. Many holy scriptures attempt to explain this universe (some make wildly incorrect guesses), but only God knows the correct answer. We are reminded of Greek-Sicilian, Pre-Socratic philosopher Empedocles' oftentimes quoted observation: 'The nature of God is a circle, of which the center is everywhere, and the circumference is nowhere.'

In this meditation, Guru Nanak explains a central tenet of his cosmological belief: the boundlessness of this created universe. It is limitless from the human perspective, but not from that of the Creator's. God alone knows the answer. All of our guesses are wild and meaningless; they are just 'not this, not this' (*na iti, na iti*) type. Instead of making assumptions, we could better spend our time putting our faith in the Lord who knows it all.

23

Divine Love is its Own Reward

Saalaahii saalaahi aytee surat na paa-ii-aa.
Nadee-aa atai vaah pavahi samund na jaanii-ahi.
Samund saah sultaan girhaa saytii maal dhan.
Kiirhii tul na hovnii jay tis manhu na viisrahei.

Devotees who worship Him know not about His greatness,
as rivers and rivulets know not about the oceanic vastness.
Kings with wealth greater than the sweep of an ocean
are worthless like an ant if their minds are not
filled with His devotion.

Spiritual life involves making hard choices. We reach the place where we set out to go. But are we making the right decision? A river headed in the direction of the ocean does not worry about its destination. It knows intuitively that it will reach its goal. The choices we make have consequences, whether we realize it or not.

There is no way for us to know the full sweep of divine power through the simple acts of prayer and meditation, particularly in the initial stages of our spiritual life. Is this an opportunity, or is this a constraint? This meditation gives us optimism. It is human nature to want to be rewarded every step of the way. If we don't achieve results in a short time, we are likely to get disheartened.

We need to remember that divine love is a reward. The river knows that eventually it will flow into the ocean. The thought of not reaching the ocean does not bother it. The same process holds for a true follower. Once we are on the correct path, we will get there. That is the promise.

Our true worth is our spiritual strength and the intensity of our devotion to the Name. A vast amount of wealth or worldly power means nothing if our heart is not filled with the love of God. A sceptic's true worth is smaller than the tiniest creature.

Another interpretation of this meditation is that, even with all the devotion, God's true greatness would not be fully revealed to us. But should it matter? When the river enters the ocean, its contents are no longer those of the river. The river's contents already have become part of the ocean. Its water doesn't ask, what is the nature of water in this vast ocean? It is the ocean.

24

Infinite

Ant na siftee kahan na ant.
Ant na karnai dayn na ant.
Ant na vaykhan sunan na ant.
Ant na jaapai ki-aa man mant.
Ant na jaapai kiitaa aakaar.
Ant na jaapai paaraavaar.
Ant kaaran kaytay billaahi.
Taa kay ant na paa-ay jaahi.
Ayhu ant na jaanai ko-ay.
Bahutaa kahee-ai bahutaa ho-ay.
Vadaa saahib oochaa thaa-o.
Oochay upar oochaa naa-o.
Ayvad oochaa hovai ko-ay.
Tis oochay ka-o jaanai so-ay.
Jayvad aap jaanai aap aap.
Naanak nadree karmee daat.

Infinite are divine attributes and their numbering.
Infinite are divine creations and benedictions.
Infinite are divine understandings and listening capacities.
Infinite are divine modes of thinking.
Infinite are divine shapes and divine creations.
Infinite are beginnings and endings.
Many have yearned to know the limits of the cosmos.
Yet this search ended in vain, without a clue.
This limit no one really knows;

the more we say, the greater it shows.

He is the Lord and His majesty and abodes are the highest.

Highly praised and exalted is His loving name.

If there was someone, just anyone, with His stature,

only then would we know the meaning of His greatness.

His grace is our gift, says Nanak.

This gift is our great treasure.

If there is one word to describe God's unrestrained power, it would be 'infinite'—meaning boundless, limitless, unbounded, inexhaustible, incalculable, and measureless. Infinite is a measure that has no specific count. It is true of God's creation (there are no limits), God's ability to see and hear everything (nothing is hidden), and God's ability to bless and redeem all beings (it is never too late to ask for God's mercy). Many people have attempted to know these cosmic boundaries, but their efforts failed. If anyone could accomplish this task, that person would have the same stature as God. This is impossible. For the most part, human beings have problems dealing with the concept of 'infinite', because it means dark and empty spaces without any definite boundaries.

For us to deal with the infinite, we have to do what the poet and philosopher William Blake suggested: 'If the doors of perception were cleansed, everything would appear to man as it is, infinite.'[1] The process of cleansing the doors of perception is a spiritual process. This is another way of saying that the infinite cannot be defined with our ordinary experience, nor does it have to be. If God's greatness is infinite, there will be no end to our description. The meditation expresses this paradox in a beautiful line—'the more we say, the greater it shows'. Think of a story that expands by the very act of its telling.

1   William Blake, *The Marriage of Heaven and Hell* (London: Oxford University Press, 1975), p. 26.

119

25

Divine Generosity and Benevolence

Bahutaa karam likhi-aa naa jaa-ay.
Vadaa Daataa til na tamaa-ay.
Kaytay mangahei jodh apaar.
Kayti-aa ganat nahii viichaar.
Kaytay khap tutahei vaykaar.
Kaytay lai lai mukar paahei.
Kaytay muurakh khaahii khaahi.
Kayti-aa duukh bhuukh sad maar.
Ayhei bhe daat tayree Daataar.
Band khalaasee bhaanai ho-ay.
Hor aakh na sakai ko-ay.
Jay ko khaa-ik aakhan paa-ay.
Oh jaanai jaytii-aa muhi khaa-ay.
Aapay jaanai aapay day-ay.
Aakhahei se bhe kay-ii kay-ay.
Jis no bakhsay sifat saalaah.
Naanak paatisaahee paatisaahu.

His generosity we cannot in word record.
He seeks not a seed we can afford.
Even the mighty seek His favour and endearment.
And others, whose numbers are beyond good judgement.
There are those who rot in evil encampment.
There are those who receive without gratitude.
And others who consume with servitude.
There are those who are victims of hunger and chastisement.

But they accept this as a divine gift of spiritual fulfilment.

His benevolence can break our mortal bond.

None can interfere with the divine plan, here or beyond.

If any fool ventures to unfold His mystery,

unlimited blows will that person receive for such buffoonery.

He knows our needs and gives to us carefully.

Only a few acknowledge this and live gracefully.

If He is so pleased to confer His blessings, the recipient,

says Nanak, will be the King of Kings!

God is generous in giving and does not expect anything in return. But this does not mean that we should fail to acknowledge what we receive. The worst sin of all is the lack of a simple acknowledgement. When our ego imprisons us, we are more likely to say, 'Yes, I did it' when we should say, 'With divine grace, it has become possible for me to achieve what I have achieved in this life.' Such an acknowledgement is the first step on the road to self-realization.

This meditation is a real celebration of divine generosity and benevolence. Such is the scope and measure of giving that it is difficult to describe it in words. God gives generously without expecting anything in return. The seekers are not only the poor and the needy, but also the mighty and the powerful. All of us need divine generosity, irrespective of our status in life. Most of us acknowledge these gifts with humility and remembrance, but there are those who are ungrateful and their behaviour shows it. They make their accomplishments look like their achievements, as if there was no divine facilitation that led to their success.

Arrogance is a fallacy in which the foolish indulge. They forget that divine intervention is needed not only for material things but also to break the bonds of mortality—the endless cycles of birth and death. Arrogant people are here for a prolonged period of suffering because they are unworthy of God's most generous reward—the gift of immortality.

26

Only the Creator is Uncreated and Immortal

Amul gun amul vaapaar.
Amul vaapaarii-ay amul bhandaar
Amul aavahei amul lai jaahei.
Amul bhaa-ay amulaa samaahei.
Amul dharam amul diibaan.
Amul tul amul parvaan.
Amul bakhsiis amul niisaan.
Amul karam amul farmaan.
Amulo amul aakhi-aa na jaa-ay
Aakh aakh rahay liv laa-ay.
Aakhahei vayd path puraan.
Aakhahei parhay karahei vakhi-aan.
Aakhahei barmay aakhahei ind.
Aakhahei gopii tai govind.
Aakhahei iisar aakhahei sidh.
Aakhahei kaytay kiitay budh.
Aakhahei daanav aakhahei dayv.
Aakhahei sur mun jan sayv.
Kaytay aakhahei aakhan paahei.
Kaytay kahei kahei uth uth jaahei.
Aytay kiitay hor karayhei.
Taa aakh na sakahei kay-ii kay-ay.
Jayvad bhaavi tayvad ho-ay
Naanak jaanai Saachaa so-ay.
Jay ko aakhai boluvigaarh.
Taa likii-ai sir gaavaaraa gaavaar.

His goodness we cannot in word record.
Unlimited are His stores and virtuous trades.
Priceless are those who are born to attain worthiness
and those who depart after attaining it.
Those who love the Lord are immersed
in deep absorptions and meditations.
Divine law is priceless; divine court is priceless.
The standards and measures are priceless.
Priceless is His forgiveness and symbols.
Priceless is His compassion; priceless are commands.
This pricelessness cannot be described.
People trying to do this have gotten tired.
The Vedas describe the Lord.
Scholars talk about them and instruct others.
Brahma and Indra had something to say.
So did Krishna and his milkmaids.
Shiva said some things and yogis too.
Buddhas who have come and gone
have spoken about the Lord.
Many godly persons and saints too have done the same.
Many who are living and are trying to do the same.
They say what they have to and then they depart.
The Lord has created many; even if more are created,
none will succeed in this task.
The Lord decides the vastness and keeps this a secret.
If a talker talks about it, that person
will surely demonstrate unmatched ignorance.

Pricelessness of the divine 'trade' is hard to describe. In the realm of the spirit, earthly measures are of little use. Metaphorically speaking, traders who come in search of godly gifts have access to an unlimited range of precious things, meaning mystical experiences of the highest order. The store of divine love can never be emptied. Devotees have the whole treasure at their disposal.

The central currency of this trade is love—unconditional love. We love God without any expectation, and our love is returned to us in more ways than we can count. The sanctity of the divine court is matched only by the paths of righteousness that intersect this sacred space. There is a precise measurement of our actions; even an ounce of good would weigh a ton.

Such is the beauty and grandeur of the divine court that all scriptures contain long descriptions of its mystical delights. Sages and holy incarnations, such as Brahma, Indra, Krishna, Buddhas of supreme enlightenment, ascetics, and demons, have all been singing praises of the One who is the sole master of this universe. This procession of sages, singing hymns of praise, has come and gone, but the reality of God's glory has not changed. Only God is uncreated; only God is immortal. All greatness, all goodness stems from this singular source. If we know this source, we are enlightened and genuinely empowered. Although not pretending to describe the unknown shows real wisdom, only the foolish would actually attempt to do so.

27

We Praise Thee, O God [*Te Deum*]

So dar

So dar kayhaa so ghar kayhaa jit bahei sarab samaalay.

Vaajay naad anayk asankhaa kaytay vaavanhaaray.

Kaytay raag paree si-o kahii-an kaytay gaavanhaaray.

Gaavahei tuhno pa-un paanii baisantar gaavai raajaa dharam du-
aaray.

Gaavahei chit gupat likh jaaneh likh likh dharam viichaaray.

Gaavahei iisar barmaa dayvii sohan sadaa savaaray.

Gaavahei ind idaasan baithay dayviti-aa dar naalay.

Gaavahei sidh samaadhii andar gaavan saadh vichaaray.

Gaavan jatii satii santokhii gaavahi viir karaaray.

Gaavan pandit parhan rakhiisar jug jug vaydaa naalay.

Gaavahei mohnii-aa man mohan surgaa machh pa-i-aalay.

Gaavan ratan upaa-ay tayray athsath tirath naalay.

Gaavahei jodh mahaabal suuraa gaavahi khaanii chaaray.

Gaavahei khand mandal varbhandaa kar kar rakhay dhaaray.

Say-ee tudhuno gaavahi jo tudh bhaavan ratay tayray bhagat
rasaalay.

Hor kaytay gaavan say mai chit na aavan Naanak ki-aa veechaaray.

So-ee so-ee sadaa Sach Saahib Saachaa Saachee naa-ee.

Hai bhii hosee jaa-ay na jaasii rachnaa jin rachaa-ii.

Rangii rangii bhaatii kar kar jinsii maa-i-aa jin upaa-ii.

Kar kar vaykhai kiitaa aapnaa jiv tis dee vadi-aa-ii.

Jo tis bhaavai so-ii karsii hukam na karnaa jaa-ii.

So Paatisaahu saahaa Paatisaahib Naanak rahan rajaa-ii.

Where is the gate? Where is the great mansion?

Where is the place for Him to see what He has created?

Countless are the instruments that make divine melodies.

Countless are the songs, and many are the players of symphonies.

Wind, water, and fire sing praises, while Dharmaraj keeps
   appreciating.

Shiva, Brahma, and goddesses laud Thee with sheer beauty
   permeating.

Chitra and Gupta keep record, while Dharmaraj does the
   adjudicating.

God Indra sings with Brahma and beautiful goddesses.

Saints in deep trance chant the Divine Name in soul-nourishing
   contemplation.

The self-restrained, virtuous, and contented join in this jubilation.

Scholars and sages laud Him in texts written in many ages.

Mermaids extol Him from upper, lower, and middle stages.

Fourteen sacred objects sing with sixty-eight sacred places.

Mighty heroes and the four sources of life pay their homage.

There are those who sing as a sign of their thanksgiving.

There are others, O Nanak, who are beyond imagining.

The Lord is eternal and so is the glory.

The Creator knows not birth and death.

Choosing different species and colours, He made this physical reality.

Beholding this creation, He provides testimony to own immensity.

His actions are not restrained by anyone's demand.

He is, says Nanak, the Supreme Ruler who is fully in command!

The City of God is the most beautiful of all places. It is the brightest and the purest of all places. It is the centre of all spiritual and creative energy of our universe. We may not be able to experience the sanctity of this place, but we can picture in our imagination the exquisite arrangement of various natural elements and the presence of gods and goddesses who are all subordinate to the divine will. It is a place of perfect harmony—creation at its very best. If the thought of this sacred place is so uplifting, can we imagine what an experience it would offer to anyone who goes there!

This is a vivid and deeply moving description of the holy realm. We want to know where the Lord lives. Where is the gate and where is the boundary wall? All the sense of divine wonder and excitement is captured in this one question. If we are divinely inspired, can our imagination succeed in visualizing something as majestic and mysterious?

The place is wrapped in sounds made by all kinds of musical instruments. There are singers and minstrels singing songs of love in ragas of unparalleled perfection. Even nature joins this vocal chorus, with the wind, water, and fire providing the background rhythms and sounds.

Those present in this divine court have prescribed roles. The recording angels, Chitra and Gupta, keep track of good and bad actions of every being. The presence of other deities, such as Shiva and Brahma, is marked. Indra is seated on His throne. In addition to these deities, there are warriors, scholars, and heroes. There are sacred sights and places, the best and the most beautiful pieces of this magnificent creation, that enhance the magical quality of the divine residence. The Creator, having created this universe, beholds the creation as an expression of the perfect love for all created beings and objects.

28

Contentment, Awareness, Association

Munda santokh saram pat jholii dhi-aan kii karahi bibhoot.
Khinthaa kaal ku-aarii kaa-i-aa jugat dandaa partiit.
Aa-ee panthii sagal jamaatee man jiitai jag jeet.
Aadays tisai aadays.
Aad aniil anaad anaahat jug jug ayko vays.

Take earrings of contentment and carry the begging bowl of
    honest effort.
Make the awareness of approaching mortality your patched garment;
let purity be a way of life, with the staff of faith acting as a deterrent.
Stay closer to like-minded associates, who are from the same
    higher world.
When you conquer the mind, you conquer the world.
Let me hail Thee, O Supreme Being!
Without the beginning or the end, living through all time.

Being a traveller on the spiritual path requires us to change our way of life. We should seek total contentment. We should be modest and make a sincere effort to channel our energies to meet our desired ends. Meditation should become an essential part of our daily living. We should conquer the fear of death by being aware of its imminence. We should spend most of our time with the same spiritual brotherhood to which we belong. This should help us in gaining greater control of our mental faculties. It is only through controlling our mind that we can make progress. Conquering our mind (ego-mind) is metaphorically equivalent to conquering the world.

Once we truly believe in God, we attain internal contentment, outward modesty, soulful living, freedom from the fear of death, and hope for atonement. Any human being searching for fulfilment must have a contented mind. Contentment must be a visible part of our life, like an ornament that is worn for the pleasure of being seen. Being modest about ourselves and our accomplishments is the quality of a real achiever. Our modesty should match that of the beggar who walks around with a begging bowl.

We should be so absorbed in the meditation of the Name that our prayer wraps around our body like a coating of ash. We need to lead a life that is free from the fear of death. We should be unspoiled like a virgin's body, doing what is right rather than what is convenient. Our greatest strength is the staff symbolizing our faith in God. Faith is our real strength. Nothing more is needed.

Seekers of the spirit should be careful about the teachers and spiritual associates whom they select. They should keep the company of truly realized persons, people who can be their guides, on the spiritual path. The meditation tells us a simple secret of living: if we conquer our mind, we shall conquer the world. What is simple for a spiritually developed person is not simple for most of us. Instead of capturing our ego-mind, we like to lead our lives as its prisoner. This can change if we persist in doing the right thing—following our path with passion and courage.

29

The Divine Knowledge

Bhugat gi-aan da-i-aa bhandaaran ghat ghat vaajeh naad.
Aap naath naathii sabh jaa kii ridh sidh avraa saad.
Sanjog vijog du-ay kaar chalaaveh laykhay aavahi bhaag.
Aadays tisai aadays.
Aad aniil anaad anaahat jug jug ayko vays.

Let divine knowledge be the nourishment, and compassion our treasure.
We should listen to the internal melody for an experience of true
   rapture.
Our Lord is the real owner of this vast universe.
Wealth and rituals are diversions, and even perverse.
Union and separation are for the Lord to arrange.
We receive what our good actions get us in exchange.
All honour to the Supreme Being!
Without the beginning or the end, living through all time.

The most challenging task for us is to take care of our inner self. That is the storehouse of divine knowledge. We may call it 'soul'. Nothing except our soul is going to go beyond to experience the beauteous vision of God. What do we need as we go? The divine knowledge provides nourishment, compassion governs our dealings with the world, and Arcadian music, which beats in every human heart, reminds us of God's presence.

The search for God is most rewarding at the start, during the entire course of the journey, and on reaching the goal. Divine knowledge provides nourishment for our inner self. We know how to nourish our body, but nourishment and enrichment of the inner self are not easily understood. What do we need to carry with us on this journey? Compassion is the first requirement. A compassionate heart alone can show us the path. We need to walk while listening to the divine melody that beats in our heart.

We need to exercise caution so that we follow the correct path. Many paths promise short-term rewards or material gains through magical and miraculous acts. Those are false ways. There is no magic on the true track, except the magic of the divine glow that surrounds and protects all incoming souls. There are no miracles, except the wonder of love that is perhaps the biggest miracle of all.

We need to remember how everything is divinely ordained. The pleasure of the union and the pain of separation are rewards or punishments for our efforts. If we reap a bountiful harvest because of our good actions, God is our protector without us ever knowing about it.

30

Brahma-Vishnu-Shiva Trinity

Aykaa maa-ii jugat vi-aa-ii tin chaylay parvaan.
Ik sansaarii ik bhandaarii ik laa-ay diibaan.
Jiv tis bhaavai tivai chalaavai jiv hovai furmaan.
Oh vaykhai onaa nadar na aavai bahutaa ayhu vidaan.
Aadays tisai aadays.
Aad aniil anaad anaahat jug jug ayko vays.

The Primal Mother, through a mysterious union,
delivered three sons, known as the Holy Trinity.
First was the Creator, second was the Preserver,
and the third was the Judge of human frivolity.
In reality, nothing happens without the True One's will,
The magnanimous saviour,
unseen to the Trinity, watches them all.
All honour to the Supreme Being!
Without the beginning or the end,
living through all time.

There is a mythological belief about the different roles of gods who are given the responsibility of creating, nourishing, and destroying the universe (thereby making it ready for recreation). Should such gods exist, they would have this power as the sons of the Supreme Creator, herein called the 'Primal Mother'. There is no power to create or destroy that is not drawn from the primal source that we worship as God.

The Eternal Being made a dramatic plan involving the creation of the world, its preservation, destruction, and recreation. The three sons of the Primal Mother, who are worshipped as gods in their own right, were made responsible for creating the universe (the work of Brahma), preserving and nourishing it (the role of Vishnu), and finally destruction and recreation (the task of Shiva). In reality, however, it is the will of the Supreme that is being expressed by these deities. Nothing is hidden from God who sees them, like everything else. There is only one source of all mystical power. The relationship of the Supreme with other gods and goddesses is like that of a principal with its agents. Agents have power as long as it is exercised in accordance with the wishes of the principal.

31

Truth in Action

Aasan lo-ay lo-ay bhandaar.
Jo kichh paa-i-aa so aykaa vaar.
Kar kar vaykhai Sirjanhaar.
Naanak Sachay kii saachee kaar.
Aadays tisai aadays.
Aad aneel aniil anaahat jug jug ayko vays.

The Creator's thrones and treasures
are in numerous worlds that hold everything imaginable.
These places were fully
and adequately stocked, once and for all.
The Creator, after having created the universe,
watches over it.
Nanak, the maker of Truth, is Truth explicit.
All honour to the Supreme Being!
Without the beginning or the end, living through all time.

Divine presence knows no limits, no boundaries. All the worlds have been adequately provided for and are under constant vigil. Neither good nor evil has any place to hide. We can feel the divine presence; yet, in many respects, it seems that we are too far away, given our own imperfections.

God's home is located in all the worlds. Divine presence is limitless. No one can escape it. The founding principle of this empire of the spirit is compassion and equity. All human beings are given a reserve of divine mercy to draw upon like a bank account. No one gets more or less.

We all start with the same balance, yet, in the end, some multiply their savings while others end up with negative balances. We may not see this organizing principle, but it operates at all times.

When bad things happen, we ask: 'Why me?' or 'Why now?' Such reactions show our immaturity and lack of understanding of the laws of creation. There are no chance happenings; everything is part of the creative design. We should wait for those rare moments of illumination when miracles happen. These flashes of sudden enlightenment can be attributed to the fact that God watches us at all times and, thus, we are exposed to the flow of divine energy. We are never away from divine guidance, especially when the True One has something to say to us—a reminder, a piece of advice. When we hear this inner voice, we need to stop, listen, and learn.

32

Prayer as a Single-Minded Devotion

Ik duu jiibhou lakh hohi lakh hoveh lakh vees.
Lakh lakh gayrhaa aakhii-ahi ayk naam jagdiis.
Ayt raahi pat pavrhii-aa charhii-ai ho-ay ikiis.
Sun galaa aakaas kii kiitaa aa-ii rees.
Naanak nadrii paa-ii-ai kuurhii kuurai thees.

If I had not one but one hundred thousand tongues,
multiplying twentyfold as a simple matter.
A hundred thousand times
I would say His name with confidence.
Such single-minded devotion
is a ladder that aligns me with Him.
The sound of the celestial song
raises even the lesser wormlike quadruped.
Only divine grace takes us there, says Nanak,
and let false ones boast and claim.

Prayer is the most effective way of making progress on the spiritual route. It brightens our entire being and gives us concentration that we can't get in the ordinary course. Prayer is not, as is commonly understood, a dry, endless repetition of a word or collection of words. Words are of least importance in a prayer. Our soul can express itself without words or in 'soul expressions' that can't be translated into words. It is like a particle of light that pierces the darkness of our inner self, giving our body and the soul purity that we generally associate with angels.

Prayer may be used for various purposes: to ask for something for ourselves, to ask for something for those whom we love, to make a confession of wrongdoing, or to sing praises of the Lord. Whatever the purpose, every prayer, in the end, is an effort to connect with the Universal Mind, the sublime source of all energy in this universe.

Even if we had a thousand tongues, the only proper use for them would be to say a prayer. Such is the magical healing quality of words that even the lowest creatures find comfort after hearing the Word. In recent years, many experiments have been conducted to test the power of prayer. In several cases, the results can't be explained rationally. The problem is our ignorance about our inner strength, the strength being a divine gift. St. Augustine asks us not to look outside, but to look into our own self as the truth lies within. This truth finds its expression in the form of a prayer.

33

Transforming Powerlessness
into Genuine Power

Aakhan jor chupai nah jor.
Jor na mangan dayn na jor.
Jor na jiivan maran nah jor.
Jor na raaj maal man sor.
Jor na surtii gi-aan viichaar.
Jor na jugtii chhutai sansaar.
Jis hath jor kar vaykhai so-ay.
Naanak uttam niich na ko-ay.

No power to speak or keep myself silent.
No power to ask or be benevolent.
No power to live or die of my own will or action.
No power to gain wealth that causes mental commotion.
No power to gain consciousness or divine knowledge, or to
    meditate.
No power to leave this world or to gain another birth.
The True One has the power to use it as our caretaker.
By our own strength, says Nanak, none is higher or lower!

This meditation summarizes our limitations as human beings. There are many things we don't control or can't do. But there is one thing we can easily do. We can choose God. By aligning ourselves with the Lord, we break the bonds of our helplessness. We can free ourselves to take part in the magic of life.

Without divine grace and compassion, we are entirely helpless. We do not control our speech because that depends on the breath of life infused in us by the holy spirit. Some people are born with a speech disability; some lose the power to speak because of illness. Ultimately, it depends on whether we are given the gift of life, a life that is complete in all respects. The power to move, to think, to speak, and to seek divine grace is all part of our enlightenment.

34

The Earthly Realm

Raatii rutii thitee vaar.
Pavan paanii agnii paataal.
Tis vich dhartii thaap rakhii dharam saal.
Tis vich jii-a jugat kay rang.
Tin kay naam anayk anant.
Karmii karmii ho-ay viichaar.
Sachaa aap sachaa darbaar.
Tithai sohan panch parvaan.
Nadree karam pavai niisaan.
Kach pakaa-ii othai paa-ay.
Naanak ga-i-aa jaapai jaa-ay.

He made nights, seasons, lunar days, and weekdays.
Air, water, fire, and infernal walkways.
Installed in the middle is this earth as a habitat for living.
Therein, He created beings of all colours and shading.
Although they have different names and infinite identities,
they are judged finally by their moral proclivities.
He is just, and the divine court is just too.
The saints look dignified and graceful.
They accept the honours and emblems.
The imperfect are separated from the perfect at this destination.
Says Nanak, we shall know about this on reaching there.

Meditations (*pauris*) 34 through 37 provide descriptions of five realms that constitute the stages of spiritual growth. The journey from 'here' (our daily existence) to 'there' (the state of self-realization) is long and arduous. Not all of us are capable of going the entire way. What happens when we travel one-third or one-half of the way? It is better than not moving at all. Also, this is a journey that might take several lifetimes to complete. In the first stage, called the 'moral realm' (*dharam khand*), the meditation emphasizes the need for moral living.

The Creator's art of creation is unparalleled in its perfection, beauty, and complexity. It includes the making of nights, seasons, lunar days, weekdays, wind, water, fire, and lower regions. In the midst of the higher and lower regions is our planet Mother Earth, which is our abode and a place for us to grow and flourish during our stay here.

Earth is also a place for spiritual and moral living, where we can make ourselves worthy of divine forgiveness and grace. This does not mean blindly following the dictates of traditional religion. The spiritual path this meditation recommends is the belief in God and the need to abide by the principles that are at the core of several wisdom traditions.

With all its diversity, this earth is best suited for meditation of the sacred name. We have clean air and fresh water. Birds and animals are here to keep our company and provide a backdrop for our contemplation.

In this realm, as in others, God is the Supreme Judge. Good deeds are rewarded. After the judgment is made, God treats us with compassion and forgiveness. Those who pass the test bear the mark of divine acceptance. Others who fail to show the beauty of their spirit are assigned tasks in the cycle of life and death. The minimum expectation is to abide by the principles, such as non-violence, compassion, forgiveness, and charitable giving.

There are two operative principles of this realm: either our actions stand the test of moral scrutiny, or we rely on God's grace and forgiveness. The entry into higher realms is based on more demanding spiritual standards, which only some of us are capable of fulfilling.

35

The Realm of Divine Knowledge and Wisdom

Dharam khand kaa ayho dharam.
Gi-aan khand kaa aakhhu karam.
Kaytay pavan paanii vaisantar kaytay kaan mahays.
Kaytay barmay ghaarhat gharhii-ahi ruup rang kay vays.
Kaytii-aa karam bhoomii mayr kaytay kaytay dhuu updays.
Kaytay ind chand suur kaytay kaytay mandal days.
Kaytay sidh budh naath kaytay kaytay dayvee vays.
Kaytay dayv daanav mun kaytay kaytay ratan samund.
Kaytii-aa khaanii kaytii-aa banii kaytay paat narind.
Kaytii-aa surtii sayvak kaytay Naanak ant na ant.

The realm of divine knowledge is the realm of informed deeds,
actions, and living.
How can we describe this realm?
There are many kinds of air, water, and fire.
There are variants of Krishna and Shiva.
Many Brahmas come into being with different forms, colours,
    and apparels.
There are planets for righteous living and saints of mighty achievements.
There are variants of God Indra, moons and suns, and solar systems.
There are enlightened yogis, Buddhas, great teachers, and goddesses
    in many attractive attires.
There are sages, seers of utmost devotion like jewels or oceans of
    jewels.
There are demons, demigods, and jewels churned out of oceanic
    commotion.

There are numerous sources of life.

Kings and emperors speaking sacred languages.

There are different levels of consciousness to be seen of the
devotees.

It is endless, says Nanak, truly endless!

As we move to the realm of divine knowledge and wisdom *(jnana khand)*, we are given access to secrets of the creation of this universe. But in order to become eligible for this privileged information, we should show relentless pursuit in our life of mystical and spiritual knowledge. This is the realm of great gods and goddesses who perform tasks that are divinely assigned. Air, water, and fire are in various stages of making. To be in this realm is like being present on the day of creation. We can watch miracles that no human being has ever seen.

Meditations in this realm are of such pristine purity that only gods can practice them. Being there gives us an opportunity to learn true meditation at the feet of sages such as Dhruv, who meditated on the most sacred mountain of all, Mount Meru. There are places that are worthy of the seats of meditation and enlightenment of gods.

36

The Realm of Spiritual Beauty

Gi-aan khand meh gi-aan parchand.
Tithai naad binod kod anand.
Saram khand kii banii ruup.
Tithai ghaarhat gharhii-ai bahut anuup.
Taa kii-aa galaa kathii-aa naa jaahi.
Jay ko kahai pichhai pachhutaa-ay.
Tithai gharhii-ai surat mat man budh.
Tithai gharhii-ai suraa sidhaa kii sudh.

In the realm of divine knowledge, there is an explosion of spiritual
    enlightenment.
There are mystic melodies filling hearts with joy and discernment.
In the realm of spiritual beauty, there is an unfoldment of
    incomparable forms.
Many splendid shapes are crafted here, which defy the usual norms.
The dramatic events in this realm, if described, will look awkward.
Anyone who tries to say will repent afterward.
Over here, soul consciousness, intellect, and emotions are finely
    blended.
Miraculous powers of great seers are divinely extended.

This meditation gives us a glimpse of the realm of spiritual beauty,
the sphere of spiritual enrichment, and unfoldment (*saram khand*).
When our spirit unfolds, it can see such beauty that was denied before.
This is the realm where our spirit is crafted afresh as a consequence
of our spiritual pursuits in this life. The spirit, which had a temporary

abode in a body, and always expressed itself through this medium, is now free to express itself more truly. The spirit is now cast in a new mould, where it exists merely as a spirit. It can enjoy supreme bliss for which we had no concept and realization before.

The use of the term *saram khand* has been a matter of some speculation, but it is a term that properly refers to spiritual beauty, effort, or unfoldment. Spiritual beauty, apparently, is not to be confused with physical beauty. It is not beauty that could be compared in relative terms. Each form is unique in its own right. This is an essential stage of our spiritual development, because our spirit resides in a human form and, therefore, gets muddied or spoiled by the pressures of living a life in a challenging world. It is not ready, as it were, for the most significant experience of all. It needs to be fashioned, or subjected, to a process of unfoldment, so that in the next stage the soul is ready to receive divine grace.

37

The Realms of Divine Grace and Divine Truth

Karam khand kii banii jor.
Tithai hor na ko-ii hor.
Tithai jodh mahaabal suur.
Tin meh raam rahi-aa bharpuur.
Tithai siito siitaa mahimaa maahi.
Taa kay ruup na kathnay jaahi.
Naa ohi mareh na thaagay jaahi.
Jin kai raam vasai man maahi.
Tithai bhagat vaseh kay lo-a.
Karahi anand sachaa man so-ay.
Sach khand vasai Nirankaar.
Kar kar vaykhai nadar nihaal.
Tithai khand mandal varbhand.
Jay ko kathai ta ant na ant.
Tithai lo-a lo-a aakaar.
Jiv jiv hukam tivai tiv kaar.
Vaykhai vigsai kar viichaar.
Naanak kathnaa karrhaa saar.

In the realm of divine grace, there is force in the language used.
Unless it is desired, nothing else resides there for sure.
There live warriors, heroes of great spiritual strength.
Their hearts are immersed in the Name in all its breadth and length.
And there are celestial goddesses, maidens, and beauties most divine.
Their graceful looks our words can hardly define.
They do not die or get robbed by the limits of their own mental confines.

Their hearts are forever filled with the sacred love of the True One.

There live devotees, who belong to different solar regions.

They are in an eternal bliss, cherishing His beauteous visions.

In the realm of eternal truth lives the formless, the True One,

whose glance of one loving grace is a source of joy and yearning.

There are lands, regions, and biospheres we are unable to comprehend.

If we start describing them, we shall never reach the end.

There are myriad worlds upon worlds in perfect alignment,

all wholly subservient, and acting precisely as per His command,

who is the creator and the sustainer.

Says Nanak, to narrate this account is as hard as eating steel!

In this meditation, there is a description of the last two realms: the realm of divine grace (*karam khand*) and the realm of eternal truth *(sach khand)*. The realm of divine grace is an extraordinary region where only the worthy ones are admitted. The criteria are not what we have done or achieved, but whether our devotion has genuinely moved the divine heart. God bestows or denies grace for reasons that are not for us to speculate.

Who resides in this realm? It is people who are active in their effort and most advanced in their devotion. These are people who have immersed themselves in Rama's name. Rama is a metaphor for the qualities of the Supreme Being; it is the name of the perfect being.

The realm of eternal truth is the central place in the whole universe. It is the source of all divine energy. Although God is everywhere, this is the most sacred of all places because of the extreme concentration of the higher spirit. Everything is seen clearly from this hallowed ground. There are continents, worlds, solar systems, and galaxies lined up on all sides for the visual pleasure of the Creator. God mandates precise functions for each of these creations. God beholds this truly magnificent scene and feels happy. Such are the hidden complexities and intricacies that to describe this realm is as hard like metal.

38

Beyond All Realms is the Vision of Enlightenment

Jat paahaaraa dhiiraj suni-aar.
Ahran mat vayd hathii-aar.
Bha-o khalaa agan tap taa-o.
Bhaandaa bhaa-o amrit tit dhaal.
Gharhee-ai sabad sachee taksaal.
Jin ka-o nadar karam tin kaar.
Naanak nadree nadar nihaal.

Make self-restraint your oven and cultivate a master goldsmith's
    tenderness.
Be informed by an awakened mind and sharpen the tools of your
    consciousness.
Allow the True One's name to be the bellows, and atonement be the
    heat and fire.
In this crucible of love, forge oneness with the Lord to gain
    immortality.
Such a sacred workshop is constructed by using the sacred word
    and earning the gift of the Lord's blessings.
Says Nanak, through the True One's loving glance,
we attain everlasting blissful grace.

In this last meditation, which is a continuation of the preceding four meditations devoted to the description of the five realms, Guru Nanak presents a design for living that is a blueprint for entry into the higher realms described earlier. We have to learn to be patient. We need to use our understanding as a way of exploring divine knowledge. With the love of God in our heart, we need to find a way of living that conforms to the moral order that is divinely established. Asking for divine grace should become a part of our daily routine. If we can win His gracious glance, our bliss will be beyond any description.

There are powerful metaphors in this meditation. We have to make continence (self-restraint or moderation) our forge and patience our goldsmith. Let our awakened mind be the anvil, and divine knowledge the hammer. God's discipline should be our bellows, and an austere way of life should be the heat and fire. Our devotion should be the crucible to melt the sacred word. In such a mint (the little factory of love), the sacred word is coined. These powerful images convey the intensity with which we need to gain our entry into higher realms.

Epilogue

A Melody of Celebration

Pavan guru paanii pitaa maataa dharat mahat.
Divas raat du-ay daa-ii daa-i-aa khaylai sagal jagat.
Chang-aa-ii-aa buri-aa-ii-aa vaachai dharam haduur.
Karmii aapo aapnee kay nayrhai kay duur.
Jinee naam dhi-aa-i-aa ga-ay masakat ghaal.
Naanak tay mukh ujlay kaytii chhutee naal.

Air, the preceptor; water, the father; and earth, the mother.
Day and night are our nurses, and we grow in the lap of a foster
  mother.
Our good and bad actions will be examined by an impartial judge in
  true earnestness.
Some of us will be divinely embraced, while others will fall further
  into darkness.
Those who worship the Name will have their suffering terminated.
Says Nanak, with their faces glowing, they and their loved ones will
  be emancipated!

The natural order of the universe is the spiritual order. Elements like air, water, and soil are our Lord's bodily extensions. These life-giving and life-sustaining forces are expressions of divine love for this creation. Without the provision of these biological necessities, our physical, moral, and spiritual life will be arduous, if not impossible.

Whatever exists in the natural world is meant for the common good. We need to be responsible citizens in how we use these shared resources. Our actions determine not only our well-being, but also the well-being of generations to come.

God will judge our actions. If we are truthful and moral, and if we have made ourselves worthy of divine love, our labour of living this life, time and again, will come to an end. Not only shall we benefit ourselves, but we may also be able to help our loved ones. This, in essence, is the spiritual ladder, a bridge to the True One's home.

Mool Mantra Meditation

Sit in a comfortable position. Do some deep breathing exercises to centre your energy. Close your eyes and focus your attention on your forehead or the third eye. Slowly recite the following words of the Mool Mantra. This meditation is highly effective, and it will open your heart to God's love and compassion. It will strengthen your values and beliefs. It will create feelings of goodwill for other beings. It will deepen your spirituality and devotion.

(Recommended time: 20 minutes each morning)

Ek Onkaar
Sat Naam
Kartaa Purakh
Nirbha-o
Nirvair
Akaal Muurat
Ajuunii Saibhan
Gur parsaad

PART III

SELECTED HYMNS
OF GURU NANAK

If I Could Build a Palace

Moti t mandir uusrah ratni t hoai jadao.

Kastuur kunguu agar chandan liip aavai chaao.

Mat dekh bhuula viisrai tera chit n aavai naao.

Har bin jiio jal bal jaao.

Main aapna gur puuchh dekhiyaa avar naahi thaao.

[Rahaao]

Dharti t hiiray laal jadti palagh laal jadaao.

Mohini mukh mani sohai kare rang pasaao.

Mat dekh bhuula viisrai tera chit n aavai naao.

Sidh hova sidh laaii ridh aakhaa aao.

Gupt pargat hoei baisaa lok raakhay bhaao.

Mat dekh bhuula viisray tera chit n aavai naao.

Sultaan hova mel laskar takhat raakhaa paao.

Hukam haasil kari baitha Naanka sabh vaao.

Mat dekh bhuula viisrai tera chit n aavai naao.

[Raga Sri, p. 14][1]

If I could build a palace decorated with pearls and gems,

---

1   The page number at the end of each *shabad* refers to the page number in the
     Sri Guru Granth Sahib.

and walls plastered with musk, saffron, sandalwood
and other precious minerals, it will quickly raise my ambition.
I will likely go astray, drowning myself in material comforts.
The Name may not find entry into my heart.

Without the Lord's love, my soul will feel burnt down.
I have asked my guru and
now I know that there is no better place than the Lord's.

[Pause]

If the floor has patterns, beautified with diamonds and rubies,
and my bed is encrusted with gems and a charming companion,
whose costume is adorned with emeralds, invites me,
making captivating gestures, I will quickly forget the Name.

If I make things appear and disappear at will
because I have gained magical powers,
it will make people afraid of my ability,
and I will go astray forgetting the Name.

If I become a ruler with a vast army
and occupy my throne issuing commands,
it will be no more than a blast of wind, says Nanak.
On seeing this, my heart will go astray,
and I will forget the Name.

Material wealth and comforts have enormous sway on our psyche. Once we find ourselves surrounded by the luxuries of life that we never thought could come our way, the impact can be sudden and it can change our outlook quickly. Ambition can then blind us. Why do I need the Lord, we might ask? What can He give me? I have the money even to build a temple or a gurdwara. These thoughts are destructive. They burn the soul gradually. There is nothing permanent in life. Wealth can depart as quickly as it arrives. Empires and kingdoms fall. Impermanence is the law of life. The only thing that stays forever is the Name. Guru Nanak reminds us that by forgetting the Name, our lives can lose all meaning, and we might float purposelessly from one end to another before we depart. This *shabad*, which is beautifully written, is nothing short of a gem or a ruby by itself.

Come to Me, My Sisters and Dear Companions

Aavhu bhaine gal milh ank saheldii-aah.
Mil kai karh kahanii-aa sanmrth kant kii-aah
Saache Saahib sabh gun augan sabh asaah.

Karta sabh ko terai jor.
Ek sabd biichaarii-ai jaa tuu ta kyaa hor.

[Rahaao]

Jaaei puchhu sohaagani tusi raavi-aa kini guni.
Sahaj santokh siigaari-aa mitha bolnii.
Pir riisaalu ta mile ja gur ka sabad suni.

Kaitii-aa teri-aa kudrati, kevad teri daat.
Kaite tere jii-aa jant sifat karh din raat.
Kaite tere ruup rang kete jaat ajaat.

Sach milai sach upjai sach meh saach samaa-ai.
Surat hovai pat uugavai gurbachni bhao khaa-ai.
Nanak sacha patasaah aape lei milaa-ai.

[Raga Sri, p. 17]

Come to me, my sisters and dear companions,
hold me in your embrace.

Being together, let us share stories of our Almighty Lover.
The True One has all the qualities, we have none.

All power belongs to the Creator.
When the True One stands with us,
there is nothing more we could ask.

[Pause]

Go and ask those happily married ones,
what made them gain the Lover's love?
They tell me: it is the gift of divine knowledge,
inner peace and listening to sweet conversations.
The joyous Lover is attained by remembering the Guru's word.

I can't keep count of your almightiness and endowments, dear Lord.
Your creations, people and beasts, applaud your name day and night.
Who can keep a count of your forms, colours, shapes, sometimes big,
sometimes small?

When we find the true Guru and follow the guidance,
we too can get absorbed in the Name.
Guru's teachings can fill us with a sense of awe,
and it can sharpen our understanding.
The True One, says Nanak, then happily melds with the devotee.

Although the true Guru is beyond our societal conceptions of what
constitutes gender—the way we define differences between men
and women—there is a long tradition in the mystical poetry to show the
Creator as the dominant male lover, and all human souls merely yearning
for His love as females, like the milkmaids who were in love with Sri

Krishna. Divine love supersedes all earthly love because the latter has a transient quality. It can come and go. Falling in love with the Lord is a love that lasts from here to eternity. In our long journey of spiritual evolution, we can take many forms and gain the affection of others, but when death walks in, it takes away all those associations. Divine love, says Guru Nanak, is permanent and eternal. It is the pathway that can lead to the much sought-after union with the Lord.

Forgetting My Lover Even
for a Little While

Ik til piaa-raa viisrai rog vada man maahe.
Kion dargah pat paaii-ei jaa har n vasai man maahe.
Gur miliaa-ei sukh paaii-ei agan marei gun maahe.

Man re aahe nis har gun saar.
Jin khin palu naam n viisrei te jan virle sansaar.

[Rahaao]

Joti jot milaaii-ei surti surat sanjog.
Hinsa houmai gat gaaei naahi sahsaa sog.
Gurmukh jis har man vassei tis mile gur sanjog.

Kaai-aa kaamin je kari bhoge bhoganhaar.
Tis sai-o nehu n kiijii jo diisei chalanhaaru.
Gurmukh raveh suhaagani so prabh sej bhataar.

Chaarei agin nivaar mar gurmukh har jal paa-ei
Antar kamal pragaasiaa amrit bhariaa aghaa-ei.
Nanak satgur miit kar sachu paavhai dargah jaa-ei.

[Raga Sri, p. 21]

Forgetting my Lover even for a little while
can cause suffering to the soul.
How can we look forward to acceptance in His chamber?

Not if He is not everpresent in our mind.
A state of mental peace can't be reached,
and the fire of desire can't be extinguished
if we don't go into rapture, keeping Him in our mind.

O my soul, keep remembrance of the Lord alive
every day and night.
Who can forget Him even for a moment?
If there are such people, their number is limited.

[Pause]

When our glow merges with the luminescence of the Lord
and when our little wisdom makes itself inconspicuous
by amalgamating with the universal intelligence,
we rid ourselves of violence, egotism, sorrow, and scepticism.
The Lord allows a union with those who yearn for such fusion.

Once I offer my body to the Lord, as a bride offers herself
to someone she marries, then I hold back nothing
and the True One is pleased.
Do not give your true love to someone who is here for the moment.
The believer is Lord's mate in an everlasting virtuous relationship.

Guru is the provider of the water that puts down fires of cruelty,
worldliness, anger, and greed.
This is the only path on which we find a blossoming lotus
filled with the nectar that satisfies our perpetual thirst.
There is no choice, says Nanak,
other than seeking the True One's companionship if we long to
     reach His domain.

If there is one theme in this hymn, it is love for the Lord that holds back nothing. The reason we are unable to offer this kind of attachment to the unknown, the formless, is our propensity to love the known who is present and who can be touched. That kind of love has its place in life, as Guru Nanak also advocates love that binds us to our families and our communities. But he goes beyond these earthly attachments in this *shabad*. If we think of life beyond this mortal existence, the only thing that lasts forever is the love for the immortal and the omnipresent.

What is the Pride of Someone Who Has Been Created?

Kiita kaha kare man maan.
Devanhaarei kai hath daan.
Bhaave dei n de-ii so-ii.
Kite kai kahi-ei kyaa hoei.
Aape sach bhaavei tis sach.
Andhaa kachaa kach-nikarch.

[Rahaao]

Jaa ke rukh birkh aaraa-o.
Jehi dhat teha tin naa-o.
Phul bhaa-o phal likhi-aa paa-ei.
Aap biij aape hi khaae.

Kachi kandh kacha vich raaj.
Mat aluuni phikka saad.
Nanak aane aave raas.
Vin naavei naahi saabaas.

[Raga Sri, p. 25]

What is the pride of someone who has been created?
Life belongs to the Creator.
If there is a gift, it can't be demanded;
it is given or it can be denied.
What can we do?

What do we control?

The True One is Truth itself, and it is Truth that He likes.

To be spiritually blind is a condition of worthlessness.

[Pause]

If you own the forest and the garden,

you give each tree, each plant a name.

Based on what is destined for us,

we get fruits of the Lord's love.

He sows; He reaps.

The sower is also the reaper.

The perishable wall of our body contains the mason within it.

Intellect without the Name—it is like a bland dish.

The Lord, says Nanak, can make a difference.

Without recitation of the Name, there is no praise, no accolade.

Guru Nanak reminds us of our earthly situation. If we had no hand in the creation of our physical form, where is the scope for pride in our body's strength or beauty? How can we claim credit for our intellect when we had no role in its creation? The realization that the Creator has all the power and the created has none is the starting point of spirituality. Our ego and our ambition can make us spiritually blind. We have to overcome this urge. There are two powerful metaphors in this *shabad*. The one who owns the garden also owns the trees. Second, the human body is compared to the wall, and if we think that we built the wall, the mason logically resides inside this wall. And death takes away the wall as well as the mason. Why should we fall for this fallacy? The recitation of the Name gives us the opportunity, as Guru Nanak explains, to free ourselves and to merge our identity into something that is borderless and permanent.

If I were a Doe …

Harni hova ban basa kand muul chun khaa-o.
Gur parsaadi mera seh milai vaar vaar hou jaa-o jii-o.
Main banjaaran Raam ki.
Tera naam vakhr vaapaar jii.

[Rahaao]

Kokil hova amb basa sahaj sabad biichaar.
Sahaj subhaa-ai mera seh milai darsan ruup apaar.

Machhli hova jal basa jiia jant sabh saar.
Urvaar paar mera seh vasai hou milougii baah pasaar.

Naagan hova dhar vasa sabd vasai bha-o jaaye.
Nanak sada suhaagani jini joti jot samaaye.

> [Raga Gauri Bairagan, p. 157]

If I were a doe,
I would have lived in a forest and devoured greens.
With the grace of the Guru, I meet my Master to whom
I am ever a sacrifice.

[Pause]

If I were a cuckoo bird,
I would have lived on the branches of mango trees.

I would have meditated on the Name.
I would have met my Lord easily, whose beauty is unsurpassed.

If I were a fish,
I would have lived in water and still remembered my Lord
who watches all beings.
My Lord lives on this side of the river
and across the river, I would meet Him with open arms.

If I were a female snake,
I would have lived beneath the ground absorbed in the Name,
And thus my fear would have been dispelled.
Happy are the spouses, says Nanak,
who have blended themselves in the glow of love
coming from their lovers.

This composition is the highest expression of spiritual beauty. Worship of the Lord is not the prerogative of human beings. Since everything is His creation, meditation by every living creature and bird is equally fruitful. Gracefully chosen words in this *shabad* find an opening on their own to enter our hearts.

The House Where the Lord's Name is Meditated Upon

Jai ghar kiirit aakhii-ai karte ka hoe biichaaro.
Tit ghar gaavahu sohela sivrhu sirjanhaaro.

Tum gaavahu mere nirbhaa-o ka sohila.
Hou vaari jao jit sohilai sada sukh hoe.

[Rahaao]

Nit nit jiiaade samaalian dekhai gaa devanhaar.
Tere daane kiimat naa-pvai tis daate kavan sumaar.

Sambat saaha likhi-aa mil kar paavhu tel.
Deh sajan aasiisdiaan jio hove sahib sio mel.

Ghar ghar eiho pahucha sad-de nit pavin.
Sadan-haara simrii-ai Nanak se deh aavin.

[Raga Gauri Purbi-Dipaki, p. 157]

The house where the Lord's Name is meditated upon,
and His devotees sing songs of dedication
is the house where you too should sing songs of devotion.
Sing songs that speak high of Him.
I can sacrifice my being
to sing songs of joy that give eternal peace.

[Pause]

The Lord watches over His creation all the time.
The gifts that He offers are priceless
and there is no measure we have that can assess their value.

The date of my wedding with the Lord is fixed.
Let us meet and celebrate the occasion.

Send this message to every home in the community.
Bless me, my friends, so that I am united with my Lord.
Meditate on the One who has summoned me.
The day of union, says Nanak, is fast approaching.

This *shabad* is a marvellous celebration of union with the Lord. The idea of divine marriage is an integral part of the mystical tradition. This marriage cannot take place unless there is total absorption in the Name and an absolute, unconditional willingness to surrender one's being at the divine altar.

After Babur Conquered Khurasan

Khurasan khasmana kiia Hindustan dara-i-aa.
Aape dos n de-ii karta jam kar mugal chaara-i-aa.
Eti maar paii karlaane tainki dard n aai-aa.

Karta tu sabhna ka soii.
Je sakta sakte kou maare ta man ros n ho-ii.

[Rahaao]

Sakta siih maare pai vagei khasmai sa pursaa-ii.
Rattan vigaad vigoe kuti mu-i-aan saar n kaaii.
Aape jor vichhore aape vekh teri vadi-aa-ii.

Je ko naao dhraa-e vada saad kare man bhaane.
Khasmai nadri kiida aave jete chugai daane.
Mar mar jiivai taa kichh paae Nanak naam vakhaane.

[Raga Asa, p. 360]

After Babur conquered Khurasan,
he put fear in the heart of India.
The Lord is not accepting any blame for sending
the angel of death, masquerading as a Mughal.
Peoples' suffering knew no limit; so much
    terror was unleashed.
O Lord, did You not feel any compassion?

The Creator treats everyone alike.
Two mighty men hitting each other draws no sympathy.

[Pause]

When a tiger kills the herd,
the owner is questioned.
It feels that dogs have attacked
and reduced everything to waste
in this beautiful land.
There is no one to care for the dead.
O Lord, You are the binder, and You the separator,
It seems You also moved away.
That is Your greatness.

If someone assumes the mantle of greatness to please himself,
in the eyes of the Lord, he is nothing more than a worm
picking and eating kernel.
But if the ego dies and the person is still alive,
then there is hope, says Nanak,
of salvation by repeating the Name.

Guru Nanak witnessed the barbaric invasion of India by Babur and his forces. These invaders, who were ruthless in their tyranny, did not feel any compassion for the innocent civilians. The presence of such evil in the world raises questions about the Lord's compassion. Two explanations are provided. Evil exists in this world. It is also true that the Lord, who is always near, can also move away. There is no salvation for anyone, however mighty, without meditation of the Name.

From the Navel of
the Lotus, Brahma was Born

Naabh kamal te Brahma upje bed parh mukh kanth svaar.
Ta ko ant n jaa-ii lakhna aavat jaat rahai gubaar.

Priitam kion bisrah mere praan adhaar.
Ja ki bhagat kareh jan puure mun jan sevh gur viichaar.

[Rahaao]

Rav sas diipak ja ke tribhavan ekaa jot muraar.
Gurmukh hoei su ahnis nirmal manmukh rain andhaar.

Sidh smaadh karh nit jhagraa duh lochan kya hei-rai.
Antar jot sabad dhun jaage satguru jhagar nabe-rai.

Sur nar naath beant ajoni saache mahl apaaraa.
Nanak sahaj mile jag jiivan nadar karhu nistaaraa.

[Raga Gujari, p. 489]

From the navel of the lotus, Brahma was born.
As a newly born, He uttered the Vedas beautifully.
Those who failed to appreciate the limits of the Lord's might
stayed in the darkness of life and birth.

Such Beloved sustainer, how can I forget You?
Only pure souls perform His worship.
Sages do serve Him by silently meditating on the Name.

[Pause]

Sun and Moon are the lamps of the Lord.
The Lord Himself is the eternal light of the three worlds.
This light destroys vanity and pride.
The believer is pure day and night,
while the non-believer is engulfed in the darkness of the night.

Perfect in their trance, they often argue.
But what can they see with their bare eyes?
With divine light in the heart,
a person is awakened by the melody of the Name,
which settles all disputes and arguments.

O, the Lord of deities and ordinary men,
You are infinite and unborn,
and there is no one who comes close to You in stature.
O, saviour of all life, prays Nanak,
save me with Your gracious glance.

Guru Nanak often makes use of Hindu mythology to illustrate some subtle points in his *gurbani*. Brahma is believed to be the Creator. But in Guru Nanak's view, He is a partial manifestation of the Lord. The Creator appears in many shapes and forms, but since He is formless and His vastness cannot be limited, no representation is complete by itself. Mythology says that worlds are created and destroyed. This cycle goes on endlessly, but the Lord of the whole universe stays away from these activities. He is the sole creator and sustainer of life. The way we get close to Him is not through mindless recitation of Vedas and other scriptures. We need to meditate on the Name with love in our hearts. That is the key to our salvation.

For an Addict, Addiction is Everything

Amli amal n ambadai machhi niir n hoe.
Jo rate seh aapnai tin bhaavai sabh koe.

Hou vaari vanjhaan khan-ni-ai vanjhaan tou saahib ke naavai.

[Rahaao]

Saahib saflio rukhda amrit jaa kaa naao.
Jin piaa te tript bhae hou balihaarai jaao.

Main ki nadar naa aavhi vaseh habhi-aan naal.
Tikha tihaa-i-aa kion lahai jaa sar bhiitar paal.

Nanak tera baaniaa tuu sahib mai raas.
Man te dhokaha taa lahai jaa sifat kari ardaas.

[Raga Wadhans, p. 557]

For an addict, addiction is everything.
For a fish, water is more important than anything.
But those who are suffused with the love of the Lord
they love and like everything.

I offer myself, My Lord, broken into pieces,
because nothing is more precious than Your Name.

[Pause]

My Lord is like a fruit tree whose fruit is food for the gods.
Those who worship the Name, they get the gift of nectar.
I sacrifice my life to You.

Although I can't see You, there is Your presence in every place.
My thirst can't be quenched because there is a screen between us.

I trade Your Name, says Nanak, but You are the source of all wealth.
When I pray and adore You, then my doubt departs.

This *shabad* draws its beauty from two metaphors. The Lord is like a fruit tree, whose produce is the gift of nectar. But this gift is obtained only through the unconditional love of the Name. The devotee is a trader who trades Lord's name for making a living. This is the only trade that is real, because everything else is transient. It is here one moment, but gone the next one. If we look upon our profession or occupation as a sacred trade, which is another kind of silent worship, it wins us rewards in this life and hereafter.

There is Soulful Music Coming from the Dancing Peacocks

Mori runjhun laa-i-aa bhaine saavan aayaa.

Tere mundh kataare jevadaa tin lobhi lobh lubhaa-i-aa.

Tere darsan vitu-h khan-nii-ai vanjhaan tere naam vitu-h kurbaano.

Jaa tuu taa mai maan kiiya hai tudh bin kehaa mera maano.

Chuuda bhan palang sio mundhe san baahi san baahaa.

Ete ves karedii-ai mundhe seh raato avraahaa.

Naa maniaar n chuudiaan naa se vangdii-aa-haa.

Jo seh kanthh n lagi-aa jalan se bahdii-aahaa.

Sabh sahi-aa seh raavan gaii-aa hou daadhi kai dar java.

Amaali hou khari suchaji tai seh ek n bhaavaa.

Maathh gundaa-ii pati-aa bhari-ai maag sandhuure.

Agai gaaii n mani-aa maro visuur visuurai.

Main ronvdii sabh jag runade vanh pankheruu.

Ik n runa mere tan ka birha jin hou pirhu vichhodi.

Supnai aa-i-aa bhi ga-i-aa mai jal bharia roe.

Aa-ay n sakaa tujh kan piaare bhej n saka koe.

Aao sabhaagi niidadie mat seh dekha soe.

Tai saahib ki baat je aakhai kahu Nanak kiya diijai.

Siis vadhe kar baisan diijai vin sir sev kariijai.

Kio n mariijai jia-adaa n diijai jaa sehu bha-i-aa vidaana.

[Raga Wadhans, p. 557]

There is soulful music coming from the dancing peacocks,
dear sister, the rainy month of Saavan has arrived.
My Beloved, Your eyes are filled with love.

Please reach out and cast a spell on me.

I am ready to sacrifice myself for a glimpse of You.

Since I have received Your love, I am very proud.

There is nothing else in my life of which I could be so proud of.

O bride, your lover has fallen in love with someone else.

Your beautifications are useless.

Your decorated bed has no meaning.

Break them and break your arms.

You don't have the love of your lover.

These bracelets and glass bangles are not worth anything.

If my arms are not around the neck of my Lover,

they will burn in anguish.

All my friends have gone to see their lovers.

I am left alone.

Where should I go?

Which door should I knock?

I may have several qualities,

but if they don't please my Lover,

they are meaningless.

I dress my hair

and pour vermilion in their parting.

But if my Lover does not accept me,

I will slowly perish in sadness.

When I cry, the whole world joins me.

Even the birds of the forest.

But my soul does not cry

though it is separated from the Lover.

I saw Him in my dream.

When He disappeared,

I couldn't control my tears.

I can't reach You, my Lover,

nor can I send someone else.
I am begging sleep to overpower me
so that I have a glimpse of You once again.
How should I reward, asks Nanak?
The one who gives me any news of my Lover.
I will cut off my head for him
and perform my worship even in that condition.
Why shouldn't I kill myself
when my Lover has chosen another mate?

This *shabad* is unique in many ways. First and foremost, it is the most beautiful expression of divine love in the annals of mystical poetry. Second, it is written without pauses and breaks. It is one straight outpouring of love for the Divine Lover. For the one who is genuinely in love and whose love is not being returned, life is hell. Line after line, that frustration becomes apparent and it rips the reader's heart.

I Look Upon Myself as
a Sinner and a Pretender

Hau paapii patit param paakhandi
tuu nirmal nirankaari.
Amrit chaakh param ras raate
thaakur saran tumaari.

Karta tuu mai maan nimaane.
Maan mahat naam dhan palai
saache sabad samaane.

[Rahaao]

Tuu puura ham uure hochhe
tuu gaura ham haure.
Tujh hi man raate ahnis parbhaate
har rasna jap man re.
Tum saache ham tum hi raache
sabad bhed phun saache.
Ahnis naam rate se suuche
mar janme se kaache.

Avar n diise kis saalaahi tisah sariik n koi.
Pranvat Nanak daasin daasaa
gurmat jaaniyaa soi.

[Raga Sorath, p. 596]

I look upon myself as a sinner and a pretender.
You are my pristine and amorphous deliverer.
After tasting the nectar of the Name
I am seeking Your refuge, my saviour.

Your association grants me the honour
which I have none otherwise.
With the treasure of the Name well in my grasp
I too gain honour and glory.

[Pause]

You are perfect, I am imperfect.
You are endless, I am limiting.
Days and nights come and go,
but I remain soaked up in the Name.
You are true and
by remaining immersed in the Name
I become true as well.

I cannot see another one
who is equal to my emancipator.
There is no one else whom I can praise.
Nanak offers his prayer:
I am the servant of His servants,
and by following His guidance
I have come to know Him.

A true believer is aware of his/her constraints and limitations. The spiritual path is not easy to traverse. It is like a forest with no visible path. There is a good chance of going astray. This is where the Name comes to the rescue. The unconditional surrender on our part, on the face of it, gives the appearance of the loss of our identity and a state of powerlessness, but it is in fact a highly empowering state. Going to the very source of all goodness, all glory, and all honour grants us strength that we need. Ego will fight and resist. But when our inner self is filled with the Name, we can overcome all resistance and break all barriers. This is the magic that never fails to show the result.

My Soul Burns Continuously

Jiio tapt hai baaro baar.
Tap tap khapai bahut bekaar.
Jai tan baani visar jaae.
Jio pakka rogi vil-laa-ei.

Bahuta bolan jhakan hoe.
Vin bole jaane sabh soe.

[Rahaao]

Jin kan kite akhi naak.
Jin jehvaa diti bole taat.
Jin man raakhi-aa agni paae.
Vaaje pavan aakhe sabh jaae.

Jeta moh priit suaad.
Sabhaa kaalakh daaghaa daagh.
Daag dos muhe chali-aa laa-ei.
Dargaah baisan naahi jaae.

Karam milai aakhan tera naao.
Jit lag tarana hor nahi thaao.
Jo ko duube phir hove saar.
Nanak saachaa sarb daataar.

[Raga Dhanasari, p. 661]

My soul burns continuously.
In agitation, it becomes prone to wrongdoing.
The body that has forgotten the Name becomes sick.

All talk is in vain.
We may not say it, but the Lord knows it all.

[Pause]

Our power to hear, to see, and to smell—
these are His gifts to us.
We talk because He gave us the power to speak.
He has preserved us while we passed through the fire of birth.
He gave us breath.

We get attached to many things in life
and these are like 'stains' for the soul.
A stained soul will find no place in His court.

Recitation of the Name that comes with Guru's grace,
is the only thing that saves.
Even if one is engulfed in sin, says Nanak,
meditation of the Name benefits all.

A person who suffers from forgetfulness and does not realize his/her mistake can become a victim of spiritual sickness. It is a condition that can eventually stain the soul. But Guru Nanak has a message of hope for everyone. It is never late to start meditation of the Name. It is an act that benefits the body and soul. It gives us clarity about the direction and purpose of our life.

In the Sky's Platter ...

Gagan mai thaal rav chand diipak bane taarikaa mandal janak moti.
Dhuup mal-aa-nalo pavan chavro kare sagal banraa-e phuulant joti.

Kaisi aarti hoe bhav khandnaa teri aarti.
Anhata sabad vaajant bheri.

[Rahaao]

Sahas tav nain nn nain hai tohe kau sahas muurat nn ek tohi.
Sahas pad bimal nn ek pad gandh bin sahas tav gandh iv chalat
    mohi.

Sabh meh jot jot hai soe.
Tis kai chaanan sabh mah chaanan hoe.
Gur saakhi jot pragat hoe.
Jo tis bhaave su aarti hoe.

Har charan kamal makrand lobhit mano an-dino mohe aahi piaa-saa.
Kripa jal deh Nanak saaring kau hoe jaa te terai naam vaa-saa.

                     [Raga Dhanasari, p. 663]

In the sky's platter, sun, moon,
and the stars are the lamps
that look like studded pearls.
The Lord, who is luminous,
draws His incense from the aroma of sandalwood.

The wind is like His fan.
His vegetation is a garden of flowers.

What a beautiful ceremony with lighted lamps
for Your adoration, my Lord!
The heavenly sound is coming from the temple drums.

[Pause]

You have no eye, but they number thousands.
You have no form, but they number thousands.
You have no feet, but they number thousands.
You have no nose, but they number thousands.
I marvel at these manifestations.

There is light, but it comes from You.
Divine light shines through all souls.
With Guru's teaching, the divine light becomes manifest.
What pleases the Lord is the only true worship.

I yearn for the honey of the Lord's lotus feet,
every day and night.
Give the water of Your blessings to Nanak,
who is like a thirsty bird (*papiha*),
so that he finds a place in Your Name.

All *gurbani* is Lord's adoration (*aarti*), but this *shabad* is specially written for the purpose. It is a celebration of the Lord's creation—celestial bodies like sun, moon, stars, and beyond, air and vegetation, are myriad manifestations of the Lord. The visual imagery presented in this composition is exceptional.

O, Naive Woman ...

i.aa.naari.aay maanra kaae kareh.

Aapnare ghar har rang ki n maaneh.

Sahu nere dhan kamlii.ei baahar kiya dhuundhe.

Bhai kia deh salahiiaa naini bhaav ka kar siigaaro.

Taa suhaagan janiiye laagi ja sahu dhare piaaro.

i.aa.ni baali kiya kare ja dhan kant n bhaave.

Karan palaah kare bahutere saa dhan mahal n paavai.

Vin karma kichh paaiiay naahi je bahutera dhaavai.

Lab lobh ahankaar ki maati maya maahe samaani.

Ini baati sahu paaiiye naahi bhaii kaaman iaani.

Jaaye puchho sohaagani vaahai kini baati sahu paaiiyai.

Jo kichh kare so bhala kar maaniyai hikmat hukam
    chukaakii.ai.

Jaa kai prem padarath paaiiyai tou charni chit laaiiyai.

Sahu kahe so kiije tan mano diijai aisaa parmal laaiiyai.

Ev kehai sohagni bhaine inni baati sahu paaiiyai.

Aap gavaaiiyai taa sahu paaiiyai aur kais chaturaaii.

Sahu nadar kar dekhai so din lekhai kaaman nao
    nidh paaii.

Aapne kant piaari saa sohagan Nanak saa sabhraaii.

Aise rang raati sahaj ki maati ahnis bhaaye samaani.

Sundar saaye saruup bichakhan kahiiay saa siyaani.

[Raga Tilang, p. 722]

O, naive woman, what are you proud of?
Why are you not having a good time with the deep affection
of your lover in your own home?
Your lover lives close to you
and you don't know it.
What are you searching here and there?
What are you searching outside?
Put the needles of fear into your eyes
as an ornamentation for your eternal lover.
Only then you will be known
as the rightful spouse
carrying his love in your heart.

An ignorant young bride is of no use
if she does not know
how to please her groom.
She can't gain entry
into her lover's stately home.
Good deeds yield good results.
Drunk with greed, envy,
and pride, she goes nowhere.
This way the lover is not pleased.
The young bride knows it not.

She can go and ask other brides
how they obtained the love of their lovers.
Accept the will of the Lord and shun your cleverness.
Keep in mind His feet who is the source of
        love and emancipation.
Do what your Lover wants you to do,
Surrender your body and soul to Him.

This is how to obtain His love.
This is what the other brides advise.

Make yourself inconspicuous,
no other trick wins His love.
The day your Lover will return your love,
you will gain nine treasures.
The one who is loved by the Lover
becomes the happy spouse.
She is the queen, says Nanak.
She is always filled by joy, fulfilment,
and blissfulness that comes from the Lover's love.
When people talk about her,
they call her heart-stealing, beautiful,
and the source of all wisdom.

Guru Nanak returns to his favourite metaphoric theme in this *shabad*—every human being is compared to a naive woman who does not know how to win the affection of her lover. He is not far away, but due to ignorance, she is unable to establish a connection. Spending time in beautifications will not take her closer to her lover. He is not interested in physical charms or how the body is decorated. To find the one who is hiding within, an inward journey is needed. One option for her is to ask other women who have already won their lovers' affections. This *shabad* points to the importance of a spiritual community where divine knowledge is shared and the newcomers gain from the experience of those who have achieved success in their spiritual practice.

O Lalo

Jaisi mai aavai khasam ki baani taisdaa kari gi-aan ve Laalo.
Paap ki janjh lai kaabalhu dhaa-i-aa jori mange daan ve Laalo.
Saram dharam duie chhap khaloe kuud phire pardhaan ve Laalo.
Kaji-aa baamnaa ki gal thaki agad padai saitaan ve Laalo.
Musalmaanii-aa parh kateba kast maih karaih khudaa-ei ve Laalo.
Jaat sunaati hor hidvaanii-aa eh bhi lekhai laa-ei ve Laalo.
Khuun ke sohle gaavii-aah Nanak rat ka kunguu paa-ei ve Laalo.

Saahib ke gun Nanak gaavai maas puri vich aakh masola.
Jin upaa-ii rang ravaa-ii baitha vekhai vakh ikela.
Sachaa so saahib sach tapavas sachda ni-aa-o kareg masola.
Kaa-e-aa kapad tuk tuk hosi Hindstaan smaalsi bolaa.
Aavan athhatrai jaan sataanvai hor bhi uthhsi mard ka chela.
Sach ki baani Nanak aakhe sach sunaa-i-si sach ki bela.

[Raga Tilang, p. 722]

I recite the word of the Lord as it comes to me, O Lalo.
Babur has brought forth a marriage party of sin
and he demands benefaction of the Lord, O Lalo.
There is no humility; there is no morality.
The leader utters falsehoods, O Lalo.
The days of the Qazi and the Brahman are over.
Satan is in charge of the wedding rites.
Muslim women read the Quran,
and while they suffer,
they are seeking Allah's help, O Lalo.

What is happening to Hindu women is no different, Lalo.

The wedding songs of murder are being sung, says Nanak,

and blood is being sprinkled in place of saffron, Lalo.

Nanak is singing praises of the Lord in a city filled with corpses.

The Creator watches, sitting alone, how people are losing their senses

while being attached to the pleasures of life.

The Lord is true, and His commands are true,

and He does everything based on truth.

The body cloth will be torn into pieces

while Hindustan recalls my word.

Arriving in seventy-eight,

they will depart in ninety-seven

and then another mighty man shall arise.

Nanak speaks the truth and proclaims it at the right time.

India was under attack for centuries, and as many as sixty foreign invasions took place between the eleventh century and the birth of Guru Nanak in 1469. Babur, who had already established himself as a ruler in Kabul, invaded Punjab and entered Lahore in 1524 when Guru Nanak was in his mid-fifties. Babur was ruthless and his forces let loose a reign of terror that harmed ordinary people. He wrote in his diary that the people of India did not have good looks, good handicrafts, good horses, and good food. It is stated that Guru Nanak was arrested by Babur's forces along with his disciple Mardana, and was presented before Babur. No harm was done to him as Babur realized that the Guru was a spiritually enlightened being. There is a prophecy in this *shabad* that relates to Babur's arrival in 1521 and the deposition of his son Humayun by Sher Shah Suri in 1540.[1]

---

1   K.S. Duggal, *Sikh Gurus: Their Lives and Teachings* (Honesdale, PA: The Himalayan International Institute of Yoga Science and Philosophy, 1987), pp. 29–30.

Bronze is Bright, But When You Rub It …

Ujjal kaihaa chilkanaa gho-tim kaldi mas.
Dhotia jhuut n uterai je sou dhovaa tis.

Sajan so-ii naal mai chaldi-aa naal chalann.
Jithai lekha mang-ii-ai tithai khare dasann.

[Rahaao]

Kothe mandap madii-aa passuh chitvii-aa-haa.
Dhathhii-aa kanm n aavni vichuh sakhnii-aa-haa.

Baga bage kapre tiirath manjh vasunn.
Ghut ghut ji-aa khaavne bage n kahii-ann.

Sinmal rukh sariir mai mai jan dekh bhulann.
Se phal kanm n aavni te gun mai tan hann.

Andhulai bhaar uthaa-i-aa duugar vaat bahut.
Akhi lori naa lahaa hou chad langh kit.

Chaakrii-aa changaa-i-aa avar sianap kit.
Nanak naam smaal tu badha chhutah jit.

[Raga Suhi, p. 729]

Bronze is bright, but when you rub it, its blackness appears.
Washing what is impure a hundred times does not remove its impurity.

The real friends are those who walk with me
and are seen standing with me.
When I need them, they are there to help me.

[Pause]

Houses and mansions may be painted from the outside,
but they are empty from within.
They are no better than ruins.

Birds with white feathers live near places of pilgrimage.
They eat living creatures, and that is why they are not called white.

My body is like a huge tree.
When people look at me, they are mistaken.
Its fruits are of no use, but its qualities are within me.

The blind man is carrying a heavy load
and the journey through the mountains is long.
I see with my eyes, but I don't find the way.
How do I cross the mountain?

Without the Name, nothing else matters.
Meditate the Lord's name, says Nanak,
so that you are removed from your shackles.

Guru Nanak looks at an ordinary ignorant human carrying a load and trying to cross the mountain. It is something that can't be done without hurting ourselves. The burden is that of worldly goods and attachments that have no permanent value. We can get rid of this burden and free ourselves. The best way is to surrender it at the altar of the Name.

What is the System for Weighing and Measuring?

Kaun traaji kavan tulla tera kavan saraaf bulaava.
Kaun guru kai peh diikhiaa leva kai peh mul karaavaa.

Mere laal jio tera ant n jaana.
Tuun jal thal mahiial bharpur liina tuun
aape sarab samaana.

[Rahaao]

Man traaji chit tulla teri sev saraaf kamaava.
Ghat hi bhiitar so sahu toli in bidh chit rahaava

Aape kanda tol traaji aape tolanhaara.
Aape dekhai aape bhuujai aape hai vanjaara.

Andhula niich jaat pardesi khin aavai til jaavai.
Taaki sangat Nanak rahdaa kiokar muuda paave.

[Raga Suhi, p. 731]

What is the system for weighing and measuring?
Who is the assayer and what should I call him?
Who is my spiritual guide to instruct me?
And who can tell me about Your greatness?

I know that You have no limits.
You are in the water, on the land,
in the lower and upper regions of this universe.

[Pause]

My inner self is the scale,
my consciousness works like weights
and I am in Your service at all times.
You are like a merchant of jewels.
I am continuously measuring You in my mind
to keep my attention focused on You.

I should know that You are the scale,
You are the measure,
You are the balance,
and You are the one taking the measurement.
You see the whole thing.
You understand how it works.
You are the decider.

I recognize the blindness caused by the low caste
and the soul that acts like a stranger—
here one moment and gone the next.
Nanak lives in the company of these transitory artifacts.
How can he attain divine realization
while living in ignorance?

Self-evaluation is a great problem for a spiritual seeker. As human beings, we are either too optimistic or too pessimistic about our situation in life. Guru Nanak offers a good solution. We should abstain from all judgements and evaluations. He recommends the path of surrender. When we embrace a new path, a new way of being, which is centred on recitation of the Name and unconditional love for the Lord, everything will fall in place. We need to step outside the circle of our self-imposed ignorance.

My Body is Like a Mendicant's Dress ...

Man mandar tan ves kalandar ghat hi tiirath naavaa.
Ek sabad mere pran basat hai baahud janam n aavaa.

Man bedhi-aa di-aal seti meri maa-ii.
Kaun jaane piir paraa-ii.
Ham naahi chint paraa-ii.

[Rahaao]

Agam agochar alkh apaaraa chinta karhu hamaari.
Jal thal mahi-al bharpur liina ghat ghat jot tumaari.

Sikh mat sabh budh tumaari mandar chhaavaa tere.
Tujh bin avr n jaana mere saahibaa gun gaavaa nit tere.

Ji jant sabh saran tumaari sarb chint tudh paase.
Jo tudh bhaave so-ii changaa ik Nanak ki ardaase.

[Raga Bilawal, p. 795]

My body is like a mendicant's dress,
my mind is the temple, and I bathe in my heart's place.
The Name lives in my mind.
Reciting the Name, I shall not be born again.

My soul is pierced by the compassionate Lord,
O, my mother.

Who can know another's pain?
Except for the Lord, I don't think of another.

[Pause]

I can't reach You, I don't understand You fully,
I can't see You, and I can't measure Your greatness.
You take care of me, My Lord.
You are everywhere—on the sea, on the land,
in the lower and upper regions, and in every heart.

All my knowledge comes from You.
All my places belong to You.
Without You, there is no one else whose praises I can sing.

All beings seek Your protection.
They leave their worries with You.
Whatever pleases You is good.
That is Nanak's prayer.

This is a magnificent *shabad* of total devotion. When we give up everything and surrender all our worries at the divine altar, life's struggle and the mad rush of things to be accomplished are over. If the Name lives in our mind, everything else falls in place.

Only with the Guru's Sacred Words ...

Gur bachni man sahaj dhiaane.
Har kai rang rata man maane.
Manmukh bharam bhule bauraane.
Har bin kiu rahiiai gur sabad pachhaane.

Bin darsan kaise jiiviu meri maaii.
Har bin jiiaara rah n sakai khin
    satgur buujh bhujaaii

[Rahaao]

Mera prabh bisrai hau maru dhukhaali.
Saas giraas japu apne har bhaali.
Sad bairaagan har naam nihaali.
Ab jaane gurmukh har naali.

Akth katha kahiiyai gur bhaae.
Prabh agam agochar dei dikhaaii.
Bin gur karni kia kaar kamaa-ei.
Houmai mait chalai gur sabad samaa-ei.

Manmukh vichhrai khoti raas.
Gurmukh naam milai saabaas.
Har kirpa dhaari daasan daas.
Jan Nanak harnaam dhan raas.

[Raga Bilawal, p. 796]

Only with the guru's sacred words,
a stable meditative state is obtained.
Filled with the love of the Lord
a human being is satiated.
Ignorants who doubt go astray and find no path.
Who can do anything without the Lord's grace?
It is something that is received through
 the guru's instruction.

O, my mother, how can I live without keeping the Lord in view?
Without Him, my soul can't survive for one moment.
This is what my true guru has told me.

[Pause]

If I forget the Lord, I die suffering from pain.
With every breath that I take and every morsel of food
that I consume, I constantly think of the Lord.
With the Name on my side, I can stay
 detached and blessed.
With the guru's grace,
I have the Lord with me.

With the guru's grace,
I have gained the Lord's ineffable discourse.
The guru as a guide showed me that
the Lord is difficult to describe in words
and that He can't be approached in any other way.
What can one do without a guru's guidance?
When I control my ego and follow the guru's instructions
I get absorbed in the Name.

Non-believers accumulate nothing but bad deeds.
Glory awaits those who abide in the Lord's name.
With His mercy, I have become a servant of his servants.
The Lord's name, says Nanak, is the real wealth of the servant.

For most human beings, it is impossible to establish a direct connection with the Lord. This is where the role of a guru comes in as a rescuer and a spiritual guide. We should, however, restrain from jumping to a conclusion that the guru mentioned here is another human being. A truly enlightened human being is very difficult to find. But there is an easy way. *Gurbani* or *shabad* that contains true appreciation of the Lord's attributes, His formless being, His boundless might, and His compassion serves the function of a living guru. Recitation of the Name provides us with a sense of direction. It subdues our egoistic tendencies. We do not have to search for anything else. We can gain what we cherish, leading a normal life.

Your Light, O Lord, Penetrates Everything

Sarb jot teri pasr rahi.
Jah jah dekha tah Narhari.

Jiivan talab nivaar suaami.
Andh kuup maaya man gaadi-aa kiu kar utro paar suaami.

[Rahaao]

Jah bhiitar ghat bhiitar basi-aa baahar kaahe naahi.
Tin ki saar kare nit Saahib sada chint man maahi.

Aape neidai aape du̯r.
Aape sarb rehaa bharpuur.
Satguru mile andhera jaa-e.
Jah dekha tah rehaa samaa-e.

Antar sahsaa baahar maaya naini laagas baani.
Pranvat Nanak daasan daasaa partaap-higaa praani.

[Raga Ramkali, p. 876]

Your light, O Lord, penetrates everything.
Wherever I look, there is Narahari [man-lion], My Lord.

Take away my desire to continue to live.
Material allurements keep me busy.

Where can I find a vehicle to cross this ocean?
Please give me a clue, my Master.

[Pause]

Those who have the Lord in their hearts,
they can find Him outside as well.
He thinks of those who think of Him.

He is near as well as far.
He fills all places.
When we meet with the True One,
our darkness is removed.
Wherever I see, I see Him present there.

There is a doubt in my mind
because I am surrounded by the the worldly attractions.
This weakness hits me in my eye like an arrow.
Nanak says, become a servant of the Lord's servants,
and avoid facing dire consequences.

This *shabad* praises the Lord like every other hymn written by Guru Nanak, but there is a clear acknowledgment of our weaknesses. The earthly attractions have a great hold on us. They are distractions that we can't push aside. Standing on the worldly shore, we wonder about reaching the shore where the Lord waits for us. *Shabad* says that one's weaknesses hit one in the eye like an arrow. This is a deep awareness of what needs to be done; something that can't wait. How many of us have that feeling—being hit in the eye by an arrow?

Where is the Mansion Where the Lord Lives?

Jit dar vaseh kavan dar kahii-ai dara bhiitar dar kavan lahai.
Jis dar kaaran phira udaasi so dar koi aaye kahai.
Kin bidh saagar tarii-ai.
Jiivati-aa nah marii-ai.

[Rahaao]

Dukh darvaajaa roh rakhvaalaa aasaa andesa dui pat jade.
Maya jal khaa.ii paanii ghar baadhi-aa sat kai aasan purkh rahai.

Kinte naama ant n jaani-aa tum sar naahi avar hare.
Uuchaa nahi kahna man mah rahna aape jaane aap kare.

Jab aasaa andesa tab hi kiu kar ek kahai.
Aasaa bhiitar rahe niraasaa tau Nanak ek milai.

In bidh saagar tarii-ai.
Jiivatii-aa iu marii-ai

[Raga Ramkali, p. 877]

Where is the mansion where the Lord lives?
How does His mansion differ from all the other mansions?
I wish someone could come and tell me something about that place.
My eyes are searching, but not finding a glimpse.
What should I do to go across this world ocean?
I cannot die while I am still driven by this yearning.

[Pause]

My pain is like the door with two panels,

hope and anxiety, while anger is acting like a gatekeeper.

This world is like a moat in which we build a house.

By leaving behind these assets only,

we see the Lord sitting on His throne of truth.

The Lord has so many names that there is no limit.

There is no one who stands on the same footing.

He does not speak, and what is in His mind no one knows.

Where there is desire, there is anxiety.

What can we then say about the Lord?

Never lose hope, says Nanak.

It is only with hope in our heart that we meet the Lord.

This is how we cross this worldly ocean.

This is how we die while we are still alive.

The Lord is formless and boundless, but is there a place where He actually resides? This is a metaphorical question, and Guru Nanak asks this question in this *shabad* and in other compositions as well. There is no answer to this question, but the question itself is sufficient to fill the mind of a devotee with awe and wonder. Guru Nanak says that we can all have a vision of that place, but first we have to cross this worldly ocean in which we reside. This is a place of pain filled with hope and anxiety. We are in a moat in which we have gathered enough material goods that work as a big constraint in our spiritual progress. This is a condition akin to living death. To break these material chains, we need the courage to embrace the Name and to change the texture of our life from being one of self-centred to one which is God-centred.

Those Who Answer the Call ...

Pichhu raati sad-ada naam khasam ka leh.
Kheme chhatar saraa-i-che dissan rath piire.
Jinni tera naam dhaya-i-aa tin kau sad mile.

Baabaa main karamhiin kuudiaar.
Naam n paa-i-aa tera andha bharam bhuula man mera.

[Rahaao]

Saad kiite dukh parphude puurab likhe maa-e.
Sukh thode dukh agle duukhe duukh vehaa-e.

Vichhadi-aa kaa kiya viichhadui mili-aa kaa kiya mel.
Saahib so saalaahi.ai jin kar dekhi-aa khel.
Sanjogi melavada in tan kiite bhog.
Vijogi mil vichhude Nanak bhi sanjog.

[Raga Maru, p. 989]

Those who answer the call during the last part of the night,
they meditate on the Lord's name.
They are ready to move with their tents, umbrellas, pavilions,
   and carriages.
The Lord calls those who remember His Name to
   His presence.
My destiny does not give me the direction,
and I'm engaged in wasteful pursuits.

I have not received the Lord's name, and my mind has gone blind.
Filled with all kind of doubts, it pushes me astray.

[Pause]

While I have revelled in merrymaking
my miseries have flowered.
This is the primal writ, my mother.
My joys are limiting, while my pain is growing.
I am leading my life in extreme misery.

There is no greater separation than separation from the Lord.
And there is no greater union than union with the Lord.
Praise the Lord who is running this show while watching it.
We receive the human body by doing good deeds,
but once we gain the life of a human being,
we lose ourselves in distractions.
Those with a bad destiny remain separated from the Lord
while living in this world.
But hope for the ultimate union, says Nanak, is never lost.

Nanak always put himself in the same category like most ordinary people. But unlike those people, material or worldly things had no attraction for him. As an enlightened human being, he never lost sight of his utmost humility. To claim that there was something that made one different from the others, he felt, was the trigger that caused the ego to wake up from its slumber. Spiritual living is the path of utmost modesty, lack of vanity or pride, and love and compassion for all beings.

I Do Not Know if Someone is Wise or Unwise

Naa jana muurakh hai koi naa jana siaana.
Sada Saahib kai range raataa andin naam vakhaana.

Baba muurakh haa naave bal jaau.
Tu karta tu dana biina terai naam taraau.

[Rahaao]

Muurakh siaana ek hai ek jot duei naau.
Muurakh sir muurakh hai je manne naahi naau.

Gur duaarai nauo paaiiai bin satgur palai n paaei.
Satgur kai bhaane man vasai taa ahnis rahai liv laaei.

Raajam rangam ruupam maalam joban te juuaari.
Hukmi baape paase khelah chaupad eka saari.

Jag chatur siaanaa bharam bhulaana naau pandit pareh gaavaari.
Naau visaarah bed samaleh bikh bhuule lekhaari.

Kalar kheti tarvar kanthhe baagaa pehrah kajal jhare.
Eh sansaar tisai kii kothi jo paise so garab jare.

Rayat raaje kaha sabaaye duh antar so jaasi.
Kahat Nanak gur sachche ki pauri rahsi alkh nivaasi.

[Raga Maru, p. 1015]

I do not know if someone is wise or unwise.
Filled with the love of the Lord, day and night I recite His Name.

O, the Wise One, my wisdom is limited.
I sacrifice myself to the Lord's name.
You are the Creator, You are the source of all wisdom.
You see the future as no one else can.
It is with the help of Your name that I cross this worldly ocean.

[Pause]

Wise and unwise are not two distinct categories.
The same person can be wise and unwise.
The inner light is the same.
The really unwise person is the one who does not believe.

Without the help of a true guru, the Name is impossible to obtain.
If with the guru's blessing, we succeed, then our days and nights
can be spent in the Lord's love.

We gamble our lives hankering after fame and power,
noisy festivities, things of beauty, wealth, and pleasures of the youth.
This gamesmanship consumes all our energy.

By giving the appearance of being wise, we stay in doubt.
We read the Vedas, and while deluded by our understanding,
we write down our own fate.

Without the Name, it is like a crop without the land,
it is like a tree sinking in the river water,
it is like a dress with a black spot.

The world cannot do without the house of desire.
Anyone who enters this house is burnt down by pride.

Where do kings and their subjects go?
Destruction awaits those with a dual mind.
Nanak is informed by the true guru
that the throne of the unseen Lord is always stable.

As a human being, it is difficult for any one person to call another wise or unwise. Someone who is absorbed in the meditation of the Name, day and night, has no time to make these kind of judgements. On the contrary, it is important for that person to have a good understanding of one's own lack of wisdom. The wisdom in this case does not refer to what we consider as 'worldly wisdom'. The true wisdom lies in one's surrender to the Name, and the lack thereof is a sense of doubt and disbelief. Winning and losing in the worldly sense that keeps us preoccupied all the time has no permanent value. When death comes, all is lost in a second. Also, the mechanical reading of scriptures is a wasteful exercise. When the heart is not connected with the Lord, when the heart is not filled with love and compassion, we do not earn any reward by being overly religious. Guru Nanak calls this world the 'house of desire', which produces self-destructive pride. If we read any history text, we encounter great emperors and kings who ruled their subjects with an iron will. Where are those great warriors and rulers today? Each one of them is no bigger than a pile of ash. The only thing that lives on forever is the dominion of the Lord. Therefore, our whole attention should be focused on achieving one goal.

There is Nothing that Happens ...

Tujh te baahar kichhuu n hoe.
Tuu kar kar dekhe jaane soe.

Kya kahii-ai kichhu kahii-ai n jaae.
Jo kichhu ahai sabh teri rajaae.

[Rahaao]

Jo kichhu karna su terai paas.
Kis aage kiichai ardaas.

Aakhan sun-na teri baani.
Tu aape jaane sarb vidaani.

Kare karaae jaan-ai aap.
Nanak dekhai thaap uthaap.

[Raga Bhairav, p. 1125]

There is nothing that happens
outside the Lord's command.
Since all beings are His creation,
what they think is known to Him.

There is nothing for me to say.
Whatever there is, it is the Lord's will.

[Pause]

Whatever is to be done,
its source lies within Him.
There is no one else
before whom I can fall to my knees
in supplication.

I say it and listen to the Lord's sacred word.
He retains the secret to all His plays.
He is the doer, He is the cause,
and He knows it all.

He creates, says Nanak.
He destroys.
He sees us all.

There is only one True Lord. He is the Creator, and He is omnipresent. He is obtained by His blessings. All our plans and all our vocations are meaningless if they are not devised by the devotee without His blessings. This is a *shabad* of total surrender. By acknowledging that the Lord is the source of everything, a devotee empowers himself/herself.

The One Who Follows
the Lord Day and Night

Gur kai sang rahai din raati raam rasan rang raataa.
Avar n jaanis sabad pachhaanis antar jaan pachhaataa.

So jan aisa mai man bhaave.
Aap maar apranpar raata gur
     ki kaar kamaave.

[Rahaao]

Antar baahar purkh niranjan aad purakh aadeso.
Ghat ghat antar sarb nirantar rav rahiya sach veso.

Saach rate sach amrit jehva mithiaa mail n raaii.
Nirmal naam amrit ras chaakhiaa
     sabad rate patpaaii.

Guni guni mil laahaa paavis gurmukh naam vadaaii.
Sagle duukh miteh gur seva Nanak naam sakhaaii.

[Raga Bhairav, p. 1126]

The one who follows the Lord day and night
and who recites the Name,
whose heart is filled with divine love,
that person will gain inner realization.

Such a person pleases the Lord.
Leaving everything aside
that person stays in the Lord's service.

[Pause]

Both within and outside,
I am blessed with the presence of the immaculate Lord
and I spend time in the worship of the primal being.
God as an embodiment of truth lives in every heart.

Those who worship the Lord stay above the filth of falsehoods.
They are blessed and honoured.

When virtue meets virtue, there is a gain.
The gift of the Name is obtained.
It is only through service, says Nanak, that our sorrow is mitigated
and it also assists us in the days of hardship and distress.

The Lord loves those who love Him. Guru Nanak makes this statement with great confidence, based on his own personal enlightenment. This is the truth that needs no further validation. Then why do we hold back? We do this because we have a different set of priorities. But if redirect our focus, the rewards to be gained are immense. First and foremost, we cleanse ourselves of all falsehoods. Truth and falsehood cannot coexist. If the Lord lives in our heart, nothing impure, nothing imperfect has any place there. When we place ourselves in the Lord's service, Guru Nanak says, all our worries and sorrows come to an end.

The Joyful Month of Spring Has Arrived

Rut aaii le saras basant maahe.
Rang raate ravah se terai chaa-ei.
Kis puuj chadaavo lagau paa-ei.

Tera daasin daasaa kaho raa-ei.
Jag jiivan jugat n milai kaa-ei.

[Rahaao]

Teri muurat eka bahut ruup.
Kis puuj chadaavo dio dhuup.
Tera ant n paa-i-aa kaha paa-ei.
Tera daasin daasaa kaho raa-ei.

Tere sathh sambat sabh tiirthaa.
Tera sach naam parmesaraa.
Teri gat avgat nahi jaanii-ai.
Anjaanat naam vakhaanii-ai.

Nanak vechaaraa kya kahai.
Sabh lok salaahe ek-sai.
Sir Nanak loka paav hai.
Balihaari jaau jete
    tere naav hai.

[Raga Basant, p. 1168]

The joyful month of spring has arrived.
Those who are filled with Your love,
they repeat the Name with great joy.
Without You, there is no one I can worship.

I am like the slave of Your slaves.
There is no other way
to get to live in the world
other than in accordance with Your wish.

[Pause]

You are One with many manifestations.
Who should I worship?
For whom should I burn my incense?
I am the servant of Your servants.

You made the years and all the places of pilgrimage.
The True One, my Lord.
You can never be fully known.
Although we don't know You,
we should not stop worshipping the Name.

What can poor Nanak say?
All people praise One Lord.
Nanak bows his head before these people,
says, I sacrifice myself unto You
and to Your many Names.

The spring season has a special place in the Indian folklore. It is the time when flowers bloom and gardens are filled with greenery. The birds come back and life returns to the fields that were covered with fog during the winter. What better time than spring, Guru Nanak says, to remember the Creator of natural beauty, the Creator of all beings? The humility expressed by Guru Nanak in such expressions as 'slave of slaves', 'servant of servants', and 'bow my head before others' is exemplary and a lesson for all devotees.

A Kitchen Made Up of Gold

Su-ine ka chowka kanchan kuaar.
Rupe kiaa kaaraa bahut bisthaar.
Ganga ka udak krante ki aag.
Garuda khana dudh sio gaad.

[Rahaao]

Re man lekhe kabhu na paae.
Jaam n bhiije saad naae.

[Rahaao]

Das athh liikhe hove paas.
Chaare bed mukhagar paathh.
Puurbi naavai varna ki daat.
Varat nem kare din raat.

Kaaji mulla hove sekh.
Jogi jangam bhagve bhekh.
Ko girhi karma ki sandh.
Bin buujhe sabh khadii-as bandh.

Jete jii likhi sir kaar.
Karni upar hovag saar.
Hukam kareh muurakh gaa-vaar.
Nanak saache ke sifat bhandaar.   [Raga Basant, p. 1169]

A kitchen made up of gold and eating in the plates of gold.
Surrounded by precious items around.
Water from the Ganges and wood from the most precious trees.
Rice cooked in milk.

[Pause]

This means nothing without the Lord's blessings.

[Pause]

You can write eighteen Puranas in your own handwriting.
You may recite four Vedas from the heart.
You may bathe in all places of pilgrimage.
You may go on fasting and perform all religious rituals.

You may be a qazi, mullah, or sheikh,
a yogi or a hermit or dressed like one.
You may be a householder performing your duties.
But if you do not know the Lord,
you are being driven around by the angel of death.

A mission is assigned to us all
and we are going to be judged by our deeds.
The foolish will always command,
but Nanak says that there is no match
for the treasure of commendations
that the Lord possesses.

There is no limit to what money can buy. That is why the rich feel
empowered. They can not only satisfy their needs, but can also

cater to their whims. A kitchen made of gold is affordable, and all the other luxuries that we can imagine. But what is the value of all this, Guru Nanak asks, without the presence of the Name and the Lord's blessings? Also meaningless are customary preoccupations like pilgrimages. Being a qazi, mullah, sheikh, or a yogi by itself means nothing beyond an invitation to the angel of death to come one day and take it all away. These titles do not confer any wisdom, and the respect these people get is a trifling matter. To earn real honour, real praise, Guru Nanak says, we need to approach the Lord who is the owner of treasures of praises.

I am the Handmaiden of My Master

Apne thaakur ki hau cheri.
Charan gahe jag jiivan prabh ke haumai maar niberi.

[Rahaao]

Puuran param jot parmesar priitam praan hamaare.
Mohan moh liyaa man mera samjhis sabad biichaare.

Manmukh hiin hochhii mat jhuuti man tan piir sariire.
Jab ki raam rangiilai raati raam japat man dhiire.

Haumai chhod bhaa-ii bairaagan tab saachi surat samaani.
Akul niranjan siu man maaniaa bisri laaj lokaani.

Bhuut bhavikh naahi tum jaise mere priitam praan adhaaraa.
Har kai naam rati suhaagan Nanak raam bhataaraa.

[Raga Sarang, p. 1197]

I am the handmaiden of my Master.
While I grasped the feet of my Lord, the life-giver,
He has killed my vanity, and my narcissism.

[Pause]

He is the embodiment of light in my daily life.
The captivating Lord has engrossed my mind with His word.

Trivial and fake is the understanding of an ordinary person,
who is wilful and perverse in his thinking.
The body of such a person is filled with pain.

When women give up their ego and become detached,
they understand what goes on in their minds.
Her soul makes a connection with the Lord
and she does not care any longer of what people think of her.

There has been no one like You in the past
and no one is likely to be Your equal in the future.
She alone is the real bride, says Nanak,
who accepts the Lord as her spiritual partner
and who is imbued with His Name.

Guru Nanak firmly believed in the equality of all human beings. He also spoke fervently in favour of treating women as equal with men in all respects, including their ability to attain spiritual enlightenment. At the same time, following the mystical tradition, he used the symbolism of all beings as 'handmaidens' of the Almighty Lord, who is the only true male spouse. This *shabad* presents a beautiful representation of this idea. For those in the society who are fond of 'finger-pointing' women's actions, Guru Nanak says that when a woman has made a connection with the Lord, she does not have to care any longer of what people think of her. She becomes the master of her destiny.

The Lord's Name is Like a Precious Gem

Tera naam ratan karam chaanan surat tithai loe.
Andher andhi vaaprai sagal liijai khoe.
Eh sansar sagal bikaar.
Tera naam daaruu avar naasat karanhaar apaar.

[Rahaao]

Paatal puri-aa ek bhaar hovah laakh karor.
Tere laal kiimat taa pavai jaa sirai hovah hor.

Duukha te sukh upjaah suukhi hovah duukh.
Jit mukh tu salaahi-ah tit mukh kaisi bhuukh.

Nanak muurakh ek tuu avar bhala sai-saar.
Jit tan naam n uupjai se tan hohe khuaar.

[Raga Prabhati, p. 1327]

The Lord's name is like a precious gem,
and His grace is like a beam of divine light.
Darkness prevails in the dark world
and, therefore, it lacks any goodness.
The world is drowned in trivia and sinful obsessions.
Only the Name can cure these shortcomings.

[Pause]

If Lord is on one side of the scales,
and the riches of all the worlds
and everything that exists in the other,
be it known that the Lord and His Name will weigh more.
But all measures and comparisons are between the equals.
There is no one equal to the Lord.
Therefore, these evaluations are meaningless.

There is a circular relationship between pain and pleasure.
They arise from each other and the endless cycle goes on.
The mouth that utters the Lord's name,
no hunger can touch that mouth.

You are the only one, says Nanak, addressing himself,
who is foolish, and the rest of the world is fine.
If the body does not produce love for the Name,
that body is a living proof of misery.

This *shabad* starts with two beautiful similes, and it keeps the same thought pattern throughout. The Lord stands apart. There is nothing in all the worlds with whom He could be compared. Only the Name could help us to free ourselves of the cycle of pain and pleasure that perpetuates misery. Guru Nanak calls himself foolish or unwise, which is consistent with his persona of a very humble human being. One thought that comes to mind is: if an enlightened being like Guru Nanak is foolish, what are those of us who are still struggling with the alphabet of their spiritual practice?

The True Guru Has No Physical Presence

Jaa kai ruup naahi jaat naahi naahi mukh maasaa.
Satgur mile niranjan paai-aa terai naam hai nivaasaa.

Aaudhuu sahje tat biichaar.
Jaa te phir n aaveh saisaar.

[Rahaao]

Ja kai karam naahi dharam naahi such maalaa.
Siv jot kanhu budh paaii satguru rakhvaalaa.

Jaa kai barat naahi nem naahi naahi bak-baaii.
Gat avgat ki chint naahi satguru pharm-aaii.

Jaa kai aas naahi niraas naahi chit surat samjha-aii.
Tant kau param tant miliaa Nanaka budh pa-aii.

[Raga Prabhati, p. 1328]

The True Guru has no physical presence.
He does not belong to a caste or community.
He is not composed of flesh and blood.
With his blessings, I have gained the immaculate Lord
and now I remain in a blissful state.

O yogi, you stay aloof.
In your meditative state,

think about the essence of wisdom
that says that you have only this life to gain enlightenment.
You will not come back into this world again.

[Pause]

If you have no merit
and you have not done anything to deserve any merit,
then take hold of a rosary
and start uttering the Name.
You will gain enlightenment, and the True Guru
will henceforth become your guardian.

By following the True Guru,
you don't have to fast
and observe other religious customs or requirements.
He takes care of your good or bad situation.

The one who lives in a balanced state of mind,
of neither hope nor pessimism,
and has good control over one's mind and soul,
is the recipient of ultimate wisdom.
This person's soul, says Nanak,
eventually mingles with the Supreme Soul.

The Lord keeps His door and His heart open to all those who come to Him. It does not matter whether they reach there after doing pious actions, or after doing intense recitation of the Name, or through any other means. What is important is the single-minded resolve on the part of the devotee to reach the only worthwhile goal in life—to gain a vision of the Lord and living in His loving embrace beyond the constraints of the known time. Customary fasting and other religious activities are useful in their own ways, but they have a limited reach. Always yearning for the Lord's blessings and living in the moment with a focused mind pave the way for one's tiny soul to blend with the boundless Supreme Soul.

Bibliography

Barks, Coleman. 1997. *The Illuminated Rumi*. New York: Broadway Books.

Blake, William. 1975. *The Marriage of Heaven and Hell*. London: OUP.

Campbell, Joseph. 1949. *The Hero with a Thousand Faces*. New York: Pantheon Books.

Cole, W. Owen. 1982. *The Guru in Sikhism*. London: Darton, Longman & Todd.

—. 1984. *Sikhism and its Indian Context 1469–1708: The Attitude of Guru Nanak and Early Sikhism to Indian Religious Beliefs and Practices*. London: Darton, Longman & Todd.

—. 1994. *Sikhism*. Lincolnwood, IL: NTC Publishing Group.

Deol, Surinder and Daler Deol. 1998. *Japji: The Path of Devotional Meditation*. Washington, DC: Mount Meru Books.

Duggal, K.S. 1987. *Sikh Gurus: Their Lives and Teachings*. Honesdale, PA: The Himalayan International Institute of Yoga Science and Philosophy of the USA.

Goleman, Daniel. 1988. *The Meditative Mind: The Varieties of Meditative Experience*. New York: TarcherPerigee Books.

Macauliffe, Max Arthur. 2015. *The Sikh Religion: Its Gurus, Sacred Writings and Authors*, 6 vols. London: Forgotten Books.

McLeod, W.H. 1968. *Guru Nanak and the Sikh Religion*. Oxford: Clarendon Press.

— (trans. and ed.). 1984. *Textual Sources for the Study of Sikhism*. Chicago: The University of Chicago Press [originally published by Manchester University Press in 1984].

Moore, Thomas. 1996. *The Re-Enchantment of Everyday Life*. New York: Harper Collins .

Osho. 2007. *The True Name.* New Delhi: Full Circle Publishing.

Singh, Gurbachan and Sondeep Shankar. 1998. *The Sikhs: Faith, Philosophy & Folk.* New Delhi: Lustre Press Pvt. Ltd.

Singh, Iqbal. 1986. *The Essence of Truth: Japji and Other Sikh Scriptures.* New York: Allen, McMillan and Enderson.

Singh, Khushwant. 1969. *Hymns of Guru Nanak.* New Delhi: Orient Longman.

—. 2005. *A History of the Sikhs,* 2 vols. New Delhi: Oxford University Press.

Singh, Manmohan (trans.). 1969. *Sri Guru Granth Sahib,* 8 vols. Amritsar: Shiromani Gurdwara Parbandhak Committee.

Singh, Patwant. 1999. *The Sikhs.* New Delhi: Image.

Stronge, Susan ed. 1999. *The Arts of the Sikh Kingdoms.* New York: Weatherhill.

Talib, Gurbachan Singh (trans.). 1984. *Sri Guru Granth Sahib,* 4 vols. Patiala: Punjabi University.

Tsu, Lao. 1972. *Tao Te Ching: A New Translation by Gia-Fu Feng and Jane English.* New York: Vintage Books.

Index